C000046259

THE food WE LOVE

NATALIE GERRELLI

For Isabella, Amelia and Lilia

*Special thanks to Martin for your constant support,
and to Mum for always being there for us.*

*Thank you to Lynda for testing so many of
the recipes for me.*

*To my wonderful family and friends for your
encouragement along the way.*

*To the talented team at Meze Publishing and
Tim Green, the photographer, for making my
book into a reality.*

The Food We Love

© Natalie Gerrelli & Meze Publishing Ltd.
All rights reserved

First edition printed in 2020 in the UK

ISBN: 978-1-910863-72-5

Written by: Natalie Gerrelli & Katie Fisher

Edited by: Phil Turner

Designed by: Phil Turner, Paul Stimpson
& Paul Cocker

Photography by: Tim Green

Additional photography: Lucy Williams-Hunter
& Natalie Gerrelli

Contributors: Sarah Haworth, Michael Johnson,
Lizzie Morton, Tara Rose, Paul Stimpson,
Esme Taylor, Emma Toogood

Printed in Great Britain by Bell and Bain Ltd, Glasgow

MIX
Paper from
responsible sources
FSC® C007785

Published by Meze Publishing Limited
Unit 1b, 2 Kelham Square
Kelham Riverside
Sheffield S3 8SD
Web: www.mezepublishing.co.uk
Telephone: 0114 275 7709
Email: info@mezepublishing.co.uk

No part of this book shall be reproduced or transmitted in any form or by any means, electronic or mechanical, including photocopying, recording, or by any information retrieval system without written permission of the publisher.

Although every precaution has been taken in the preparation of this work, the publisher and author assume no responsibility for errors or omissions. Neither is any liability assumed for damages resulting from the use of this information contained herein.

OUR STORY

A Love of Food

I love food and so do my family. Food is never far from our thoughts. Mealtimes are important occasions throughout our days, months and years. Sometimes it's a quick pit-stop between work and play, at other times a welcome recharge with friends and family. It is always my aim to create food that is appealing, tasty and nourishing for all of us.

The recipes within this book are for the dishes that I've enjoyed making in my kitchen over the past ten years and more for my family and friends. I wanted to document these favourites as a family keepsake for when our girls fly the nest, as a reminder of home and of the food we love.

This book has taken years of writing, tasting, re-tasting and talking about (not to mention piles of groceries and mountains of washing-up) but I hope my efforts will be appreciated and well digested for years to come.

Family & Home

Years ago my husband Martin and I decided to move closer to my family home and the rolling green hills of the Derbyshire Dales. We had two tiny daughters and another on the way, so were keen to find a family-size space for us to grow into. We'd been living close to the beautiful Cotswolds for a while and loved the honey-coloured stone buildings and mild climate there, but I missed the steep hills dotted with sheep and rocky limestone and wanted a winter with white frosts that I remembered from my childhood. The home we found for our family was a beautiful old stone Engine House, part of an old lead mine, already renovated but in need of a good deal of tender loving care. We redesigned the kitchen and dining room to make a large family space and then chose fruit trees for the garden and herbs for pots and culinary use.

Over the years the kitchen has become a warm, friendly hub, the centre of family life and the perfect place for cooking, eating and nurturing. The garden has matured into a relaxed, natural space in which we enjoy family time and outside dining.

I have always loved food and cookery. My childhood memories are filled with the aromas of Mum's homemade bread at teatime and our purple-stained fingers from blackberry picking in the autumn. Growing up, my mum gave my brother and I a deep appreciation and respect for good food. She was always on a tight budget, so used her ingredients and resources wisely. She always baked her own bread and this is something she still loves to do. From her we learnt how to eat well and stay healthy and this fuelled my passion to learn more about food.

It was while studying Food Science at Nottingham University and through a mutual love of food that Martin and I met. Good food, always at the heart of our family life, is entwined in all our fondest memories.

In my early career as a Food Development Technologist a kitchen was my main office, where I worked with chefs and home economists to create new and exciting food products. Building on this experience, I studied further and

stepped into the fascinating world of nutrition and health before devoting my time and energies to our family, home and food.

Before we had the girls I would spend hours at a weekend preparing, cooking and serving ambitious dinner parties for friends and family. These days I need to make double the amount of food in a fraction of the time. Consequently my recipe choices have to be easy to prepare and cook, often in advance, and really do need to be tasty, appealing and nourishing for a growing family.

The girls have always been very well-behaved 'guinea pigs' for my recipe creations and through this have developed a very open-minded and healthy attitude to food and eating well. I am very proud of this, as I strongly believe that an understanding of food, cookery and basic nutrition is important to every one of us throughout life.

The years that I spent working with herbs and spices, and my knowledge of nutrition, have given me an appreciation for flavour in my cooking and the health-giving benefits that many ingredients add to our diet. I am conscientious about bringing a variety of ingredients to our meals and snacks. As a family we have a range of preferences in our food choices; some of us like more plant-based meals and others enjoy meat dishes so my recipes are adaptable and varied. My aim is always to make food that helps my family to grow and enjoy life. Food can make us feel good, whether it's a nourishing breakfast to start the day, a freshly baked cake or a hearty dinner to share.

The Creative Process

I love cookery books and over the years I've tried many recipes created by other people. I often adapt them to suit my needs, usually simplifying or adding more nutritious ingredients. Our favourite recipes, the ones that I've made time and time again, are included in this book. I've also included some recipes from my mother, mother-in-law and friends who love to cook. However, my usual process for recipe creation, a nod to my years in new product development, is to start with what I have in the fridge, what I see on the local market stalls or what I find in the shops. I consider who I'm catering for and the timing or occasion and then combine all this with ideas from my store cupboard staples and herbs from the garden to create something new. The seasons greatly influence my mood and desire for different flavours and foods. Travel and eating out have also had a big influence on my cooking: I particularly love flavours from the Mediterranean, northern Africa and the Americas, but I also value our great British cuisine and produce immensely.

Despite our lovely Italian surname, my husband's family do not have any remaining connections with the country itself, as they are generations removed from the Milanese sculptor who travelled over to London in the late 1700s. The family tree is a very interesting read! I'm happy to say that the extended family warmth and a great love of good food persists: family gatherings always centre around delicious home-cooked food, as they do in many countries around the world. A number of my recipes do have an Italian or Mediterranean theme because we just love the flavours and style of this food.

Happy Cooking, Natalie x

GOOD MORNING...
BREAKFAST & BRUNCH

I love breakfast. It's arguably my favourite meal of the day, particularly at weekends or on holiday when we don't need to rush. I make an effort to provide a tempting meal for those sleepy heads who need to be coaxed out of bed! For me, to start the morning with a nourishing breakfast really adds to a positive outlook for the day ahead.

WARMING PORRIDGE WITH
ALMONDS & BERRY COMPOTE

BAKED APPLES WITH HAZELNUTS, YOGHURT & HONEY

OAT PORRIDGE WITH DATES,
WALNUTS & BROWN SUGAR

OVEN-BAKED MUSHROOMS, HALLOUMI
& TOMATOES ON SOURDOUGH TOAST

SPINACH & CHEESE SCRAMBLE

EGGY BREAD WITH CINNAMON SUGAR

BREAKFAST POTATO OMELETTE

BIG FLUFFY PANCAKES

DROP SCONES WITH BACON,
BLUEBERRIES & MAPLE SYRUP

BANANA & CHOC CHIP DROP SCONES

FRESH FRUIT MILKSHAKE

APRICOT & CREAM CHEESE PASTRIES

PINEAPPLE & LIME MARMALADE

WARMING PORRIDGE WITH ALMONDS & BERRY COMPOTE

SERVES 4

This is a delicious, warming breakfast. Adding ground almonds and almond milk to the oats gives the porridge extra creaminess and nutrition. The berry compote can be made in advance.

INGREDIENTS

100g porridge oats

4 tbsp ground almonds

500ml almond milk or water

200g berries, defrosted if frozen (raspberries, blackberries, blueberries, cherries & blackcurrants all work well)

1 tbsp sugar, if needed

1 tbsp flaked almonds

Drizzle of runny honey

METHOD

You will need a medium-size saucepan for the porridge and another pan or microwaveable bowl for the berries. Make sure the berries have defrosted if they were frozen.

Put the oats, almonds and milk or water into your saucepan. Cook on a low heat, stirring well until thick and creamy. This only takes a few minutes. Add extra milk or water if needed.

Gently warm the berries either in a pan or a bowl in the microwave, adding the sugar to your taste. Stir them to dissolve the sugar.

Serve the hot porridge topped with warm berry compote, flaked almonds and a drizzle of your favourite runny honey.

BAKED APPLES WITH HAZELNUTS, YOGHURT & HONEY

SERVES 4

Fluffy sweet apple and crunchy, honeyed nuts are a delight. I make these for brunch when we have a little more time. Slowly baking the apples intensifies their flavour and preserves their shape. Serve with thick natural yoghurt.

INGREDIENTS

4 large cooking apples (Bramleys or another cooking variety)

1 tsp butter, to grease the dish

60-80g hazelnuts, halved or roughly chopped

2 tbsp runny honey

Thick natural yoghurt, to serve

METHOD

You will need an ovenproof dish or baking tray approximately 22 by 22cm and about 5cm deep. Preheat the oven to Gas Mark 4 or 180°c.

Start by washing the apples then remove their cores. This can be done with an apple corer or sharp knife but try to remove all the hard pieces from inside the apples while keeping them in one piece!

Next, grease the ovenproof dish or baking tray with butter and put the apples in. Pack the hazelnuts into the holes in the centre of the apples, dividing them equally.

Drizzle the honey equally over the apples, making sure it soaks down to cover the nuts too. Bake in the preheated oven for 40 to 50 minutes. Carefully turn the apples around in the dish halfway through the cooking time to ensure an even texture.

The apples should keep their round shape, not collapse, and have a tender but fluffy texture. Test for doneness by sticking a sharp knife or skewer into the base of the apples. The honey will start to caramelise the nuts on top.

Remove the baked apples from the oven when done and allow them to cool for a minute before serving with thick yoghurt and another drizzle of honey.

OAT PORRIDGE WITH DATES, WALNUTS & BROWN SUGAR

SERVES 4

I first ate this porridge for breakfast on holiday at a beautiful guest house in Devon. I loved it so much that I just had to recreate it at home! I particularly enjoy it on cold, blustery mornings to warm me from within.

INGREDIENTS

100g porridge oats

500ml milk or water

50g dried dates, pitted and chopped

Handful of walnut pieces

Sprinkle of soft light brown sugar

METHOD

You will need a medium-size saucepan. For best results, but only if you have time, soak the chopped dried dates in just enough water to cover them overnight or for at least 1 hour.

Put the oats in a pan then add the milk or water and the dates. Cook on a gentle heat, stirring until thickened. The dates should 'melt down' into the oats and give the porridge a rich, sweet flavour.

Serve in warm bowls, sprinkled with the walnut pieces and brown sugar.

OVEN-BAKED MUSHROOMS, HALLOUMI & TOMATOES ON SOURDOUGH TOAST

SERVES 4

This dish gives your taste buds everything. The salty cheese, sweet ripe tomatoes, toasted sourness of the bread and rich earthiness of the mushrooms. It's an easy 'breakfast bruschetta' as everything goes in the oven to cook.

INGREDIENTS

2-3 tbsp rapeseed oil

4 large flat field mushrooms

225g (1 pack) halloumi cheese

2 large ripe tomatoes

Freshly ground black pepper

4 thick slices of sourdough bread

Small handful of fresh parsley, chopped

METHOD

Start by preheating the oven to Gas Mark 4 or 180°c. Lightly oil two baking trays. Wipe the mushrooms clean, slice the halloumi cheese into eight pieces and cut the tomatoes in half horizontally.

Put the mushrooms, halloumi and tomatoes onto the oiled baking trays (tomatoes cut side upwards, mushrooms stalk facing up). Drizzle lightly with oil and sprinkle with black pepper.

Bake for 15 to 20 minutes in the preheated oven, checking and turning the slices of halloumi over halfway through. In the meantime, toast the sourdough bread then drizzle with oil on a serving plate.

Once the mushrooms and tomatoes are soft and juicy and the halloumi is golden brown, remove the trays from the oven.

To serve

Pile two pieces of cheese onto each slice of sourdough toast, then a mushroom and a tomato half. Drizzle with the remaining oil and any cooking juices from the trays, grind over some fresh black pepper and sprinkle with fresh parsley.

SPINACH & CHEESE SCRAMBLE

SERVES 4

This is a very easy, tasty breakfast dish full of goodness. I sometimes add a little smoked salmon instead of the cheese.

INGREDIENTS

1 tbsp vegetable oil

6 eggs

2 tbsp milk

Black pepper

40-50g (or two large handfuls) baby spinach leaves

50-60g mature cheddar cheese, grated

1 tbsp fresh basil or parsley leaves, chopped (optional)

METHOD

Heat the oil in a large frying pan on a low to medium heat. Crack the eggs into a bowl and whisk lightly with the milk and a grind or two of black pepper.

Pour the eggs into the hot pan followed by the spinach leaves. Stir a little with a wooden spoon then sprinkle the cheese over the top, followed by the herbs if you're using them.

Cook for a few minutes, stirring gently once or twice to make a 'scrambled' texture. The spinach will wilt and the cheese will melt, but don't overcook the eggs otherwise they will turn rubbery.

Serve the scramble hot from the pan with toast.

EGGY BREAD WITH CINNAMON SUGAR

SERVES 4

This recipe is perfect for using up stale bread. It's best to have a slightly firm, dry texture for soaking up the eggy mixture. Do use butter for frying as it gives delicious, crispy, browned edges.

INGREDIENTS

4 thick slices of bread

4 eggs

2 tbsp milk

15g butter

½ tbsp vegetable oil

25g caster sugar

1 tsp ground cinnamon

Slices of ripe pear or apple, to serve

METHOD

Start by putting the bread slices on a board and cutting off the harder outer crusts, then divide each slice in half. Take a shallow bowl and beat the eggs together with the milk.

Melt the butter and oil in a frying pan or hot griddle plate. Keep the heat on medium so the butter doesn't burn. Slice by slice, immerse the bread in the eggy mixture to cover both sides, then carefully drop into the hot pan to cook. I use a large fork and palette knife to help with this. Turn each slice to brown and cook on both sides. Transfer to a warmed serving plate while you finish frying the rest.

Stir the caster sugar and cinnamon together in a small bowl until well mixed. Serve the warm eggy bread sprinkled with the cinnamon sugar and fresh pear or apple slices.

BREAKFAST POTATO OMELETTE

SERVES 4

This is a great recipe for using up leftover boiled potatoes. If you want to include meat, small pieces of bacon or black pudding are tasty additions; cook these in the pan with the pepper. The pinch of chilli and tangy cheese really wake up your taste buds.

INGREDIENTS

1 tbsp vegetable oil

200g cooked potatoes, skin on

½ a green pepper, thinly sliced

4 large eggs

2 tbsp milk

Pinch of red chilli flakes or cayenne pepper

Salt and black pepper

8-10 cherry or baby plum tomatoes, halved

50g mature, tangy, hard cheese (cheddar, Lancashire, Wensleydale)

METHOD

Start by heating the oil in a large frying pan and cutting the potatoes into bite-size pieces. Add the pepper and fry for a minute or two, then add the diced potato and stir to coat with oil.

In a small bowl or jug beat the eggs with the milk, chilli or cayenne and a pinch of salt and black pepper. Add this to the hot pan and continue to cook on a medium heat. Meanwhile, prepare the tomatoes and grate or crumble the cheese.

Scatter the tomatoes over the egg and potato mixture, followed by the cheese. Add more black pepper if you like. Cook until the tomatoes have softened a little and the egg is firm but not dry.

If you prefer a browned top on the omelette then put the pan under a hot grill for a minute or two.

Serve with toast.

BIG FLUFFY PANCAKES

SERVES 4-8

This recipe makes four large thick pancakes; mine are about 15cm in diameter and 1.5cm deep. You can make six to eight smaller thick pancakes if you need. They really fill you up for a busy day ahead and are always tasty. If you have more than one frying pan, double up to cook them quicker.

INGREDIENTS

200g self-raising flour

50g wholemeal flour

1 tbsp baking powder

1 tsp caster sugar

Pinch of fine salt

300ml semi-skimmed milk

2 eggs

3 tbsp (45ml) vegetable oil, plus extra for frying

Fresh fruit, honey, chopped nuts, creme fraiche or yoghurt to serve

METHOD

Weigh the flours and baking powder into a bowl. Stir in the sugar and salt. In a measuring jug, beat the milk and eggs together then add the oil.

Lightly oil then preheat the frying pan, or use two pans if you have them. Pour the wet ingredients over the dry mixture and mix together gently but swiftly with a large metal spoon. Leave the mixture lumpy; if you try to make the batter smooth you will have flat rather than fluffy pancakes!

Put two large spoonfuls, or two ladles, of the lumpy batter into the hot pan. Use a quarter of the total mixture for each pancake, unless you're making smaller ones. The lumps will go away as the batter heats up.

Cook on a medium heat until bubbles appear on the surface, the sides start to set and the base is firm. Using a wide palette knife, check the underside of the pancake for a golden brown colour then flip carefully to cook the other side.

Once the pancake is cooked through, transfer to a warm serving plate. Repeat this process until all the batter is used. Note that the longer this batter is left the more it will thicken and bubble, so use it up as quickly as you can.

Serve the pancakes with fresh fruit of your choice, a drizzle of honey, chopped nuts and a dollop of creme fraiche or yoghurt.

DROP SCONES WITH BACON, BLUEBERRIES & MAPLE SYRUP

MAKES 8-10

I remember these scrumptious little spongy 'pancakes' from my childhood. Mum would make piles of them for my brother and I at breakfast or teatime. We would simply spread them with butter and sometimes jam or honey. We love them, so I tend to make double the quantity.

INGREDIENTS

200g self-raising flour

½ tsp baking powder

Pinch of salt

1 tbsp caster sugar

2 eggs

125ml milk

Vegetable oil

Thinly sliced bacon, fresh blueberries and maple syrup to serve

METHOD

Weigh the flour, baking powder, salt and sugar into a large bowl and stir to combine. Beat the eggs and milk together in a small jug or bowl then add the mixture to the dry ingredients.

Mix well to make a thick batter, and don't worry about a few small lumps. Heat a large, lightly oiled, non-stick frying pan, crepe pan or griddle plate.

Gently drop heaped tablespoons of batter onto the heated pan. When bubbles appear on the surface and the underside is lightly browned, turn over with a palette knife to finish cooking.

Transfer the cooked drop scones to a warm serving plate and repeat until all the batter is used up.

Grill the thinly sliced bacon until crispy then serve with the blueberries and maple syrup.

BANANA & CHOC CHIP DROP SCONES

MAKES 10-12

This recipe has one of our favourite flavour combinations and is great for using up overripe bananas. They are delicious served warm on their own but even better with a dollop of creme fraiche or yoghurt and some fresh berries.

INGREDIENTS

200g self-raising flour

20g soft light brown sugar

Pinch of salt

2 eggs

4 tbsp (60ml) milk

2 medium-size or 1 large ripe banana (approx. 150g)

50g dark chocolate chips

Vegetable oil

METHOD

Firstly weigh the flour, sugar and salt into a large bowl then stir to combine. In a jug or smaller bowl, lightly beat the eggs and milk together. Peel and mash the ripe banana in a large mug with the back of a fork to a lumpy consistency.

Add the egg mixture, mashed banana and chocolate chips to the dry ingredients in the large bowl and stir everything together to make a thick, lumpy batter.

Heat a large frying pan, crepe pan or griddle plate greased with a little vegetable oil to a medium temperature. Gently drop heaped tablespoons of batter onto the heated pan. When bubbles appear on the surface and the underside is lightly browned, turn over with a palette knife to finish cooking. The chocolate chips will melt a little.

Transfer the cooked, lightly browned drop scones to a warm serving plate and repeat until all the batter mixture is used up. Serve warm with a dollop of creme fraiche or thick yoghurt and some fresh berries.

FRESH FRUIT MILKSHAKE

MAKES 1 LITRE

A delicious drink for breakfast or brunch, particularly if you're short of time. Use any combination of fresh, frozen or tinned fruit that you like and honey or fruit cordial to sweeten. I like to use up soft, overripe fruit in these milkshakes. Halve the quantity if you have a smaller crowd.

INGREDIENTS

300g soft fruit (try raspberry, peach and mango or blueberry and banana)

600-700ml cold milk

2-3 tbsp runny honey or fruit cordial (try raspberry, elderflower or blackcurrant)

METHOD

Put all the ingredients into a large jug and blend until smooth with a hand blender. Taste and add more sweetness with honey or cordial if needed, as some berries can be quite sour.

Serve in long glasses with coloured straws.

APRICOT & CREAM CHEESE PASTRIES

SERVES 6

Light puff pastry with fruity apricot pieces and creamy cheese make a delightful, not-too-sweet combination. My idea for this came from a breakfast baguette topping I often make for myself on holiday in France. That version is tangy yet sweet apricot conserve with creamy, ripe camembert. Unusual and probably not authentic, but delicious!

INGREDIENTS

375g puff pastry, ready-rolled

100g cream cheese

60g apricot conserve or jam

6 apricot halves, fresh or tinned in fruit juice

15g flaked almonds

20g unsalted butter, melted

METHOD

Line a large baking tray with greaseproof paper and preheat the oven to Gas Mark 5 or 190°c.

Firstly, cut the ready-rolled puff pastry oblong (it should be approximately 38 by 26cm) into six squares of equal size. With a small spoon, stir the cream cheese to make it soft, then divide it equally between the pastry squares, placing it in the centre of each one. With the back of the spoon spread the cream cheese diagonally from one corner to the other of each pastry square.

Next, take a small spoonful of the apricot conserve and layer it over the cream cheese, again dividing it equally between the six. Place one apricot half, drained well if you are using tinned, in the middle of each pastry square then sprinkle generously with flaked almonds.

Now take opposite corners of the pastry squares and fold them over into the middle so that they overlap, leaving the two remaining corners flat with some of the filling showing. Brush the pastry well with the melted butter, using it to help the corners stick together in the middle if needed.

Carefully transfer the pastries onto the lined baking tray and bake for 20 minutes in the preheated oven until risen and golden. Leave them to cool a little then dust with icing sugar and serve warm.

PINEAPPLE & LIME MARMALADE

MAKES 3-4 JARS (300G EACH)

I wanted to make an easy, tangy, tropical marmalade and I think the flavours of pineapple and zesty lime in this recipe really hit the spot. A jam sugar with added pectin is needed to help the marmalade set. Using tinned, crushed or pre-cut pineapple pieces saves time but I prefer a combination of fresh and tinned.

INGREDIENTS

550g-600g pineapple, fresh or tinned

4 unwaxed limes

500g jam sugar, with added pectin

METHOD

You will need three or four medium-size glass jam jars with lids, or sturdy heatproof plastic pots with lids, and a large saucepan or preserving pan. Wash the jam jars or plastic pots and lids thoroughly in hot, soapy water, then dry well and keep them in a warm place.

If you are using fresh pineapple, cut off the fibrous skin, any little brown 'dimples' and the hard central core. Chop the flesh into very small but chunky pieces. Save any juice that escapes too. Put all of this into the pan. If you're using tinned pineapple, drain off the juice then chop into smaller, randomly shaped pieces and add to the pan.

Wash the limes then remove the zest with a sharp knife or parer. Cut it into thin strands and add to the pan. Cut each lime in half and squeeze the juice out into the pan, approximately 175ml.

Add the sugar to the pan then cook on a medium heat, stirring gently for a minute or two to allow the sugar to dissolve. Turn up the heat and bring to a slow boil. Simmer uncovered for 20 to 30 minutes to reduce the liquid by about one third.

Test the marmalade for setting thickness after 20 minutes by putting a teaspoonful of the hot marmalade onto a cold saucer. Let it cool; if it forms a skin on the surface and thickens up then it's ready. If it's still too runny then carry on simmering and test again in 5 minutes. The greater the quantity of juice, the longer it takes to reduce and thicken the marmalade.

Remove the pan from the heat then very carefully ladle the marmalade into the warm jars or pots. Put the lids on tightly and leave to cool before labelling. The lids should have a 'dimple' in the middle once cool. This means a vacuum has been achieved and the jar will store safely in a cool, dry place for a year. If you've used plastic pots they may not store for quite as long as glass jars. In any case, once opened, store your marmalade in the fridge.

BAKED...
BISCUITS, CAKES & BREADS

The aroma of freshly baked treats welcoming you home after a long day at work or school is hard to beat. Here are my favourite biscuits and cakes for coffee or teatime and easy, savoury breads to accompany any meal.

SEA SALT & BUTTER BISCUITS

ALMOND & ORANGE MACAROONS

GINGERBREAD BISCUITS WITH ROYAL ICING

MOCHA BROWNIES

RHUBARB & HONEY MUFFINS

VERY LEMONY DRIZZLE CAKE

ITALIAN-STYLE PLUM CAKE

CINNAMON SWIRL CAKE

CHEESE SCONES

CHOCOLATE, HAZELNUT & OAT COOKIES

EASY ROSEMARY & SEA SALT 'FOCACCIA'

WHOLEMEAL SODA BREAD

RUSTIC BREAD ROLLS

SEA SALT & BUTTER BISCUITS

MAKES 20

Sweet, salty and buttery with a crumbly texture, these easy rolled biscuits are perfect with a nice cup of tea. I sometimes make them up to the 'dough log' stage and keep them in the fridge, then cut and bake as I need them. Warm, freshly baked biscuits are hard to resist!

INGREDIENTS

125g unsalted butter, softened

100g icing sugar, sieved

½ tsp fine sea salt

1 egg yolk

¼ tsp vanilla extract

200g plain flour, plus extra for rolling out

1 tbsp cornflour

METHOD

Preheat the oven to Gas Mark 4 or 180°c and line two baking trays with greaseproof paper or baking parchment.

Put the soft butter, icing sugar and sea salt in a medium-size bowl. Combine well with a wooden spoon, then beat in the egg yolk and vanilla.

Sieve the flour and cornflour over the butter mixture and mix well until a soft, dry ball of dough is formed. You may need to bring the mixture together gently with floured hands at this point.

Cut another piece of greaseproof paper, approximately 35 by 20cm, and transfer the dough onto it. Roll the dough into a smooth round log shape, using the greaseproof paper to help you, until it's approximately 30cm long. If the dough log feels warm and too soft at this stage, transfer it to a cool place or the fridge for 20 minutes or so until it has hardened enough to handle.

Unwrap the dough and use a sharp knife to cut about 20 evenly-sized discs from the roll. Neaten them with your fingers then place the discs onto the lined baking trays. Gently indent each one with the prongs of a small fork, creating lines or dots, for detail.

Bake in the oven for 10 to 15 minutes until golden brown. These biscuits spread just a little bit during baking. Take out and leave to cool a little on the trays before transferring to a wire rack.

Store in an airtight container if you have any left!

ALMOND & ORANGE MACAROONS

MAKES 20

These lovely light, sweet treats originated in Italy. They have a slightly sticky, chewy outer crust and soft spongy centre enhanced by fragrant orange zest. Delicious with a cup of strong black coffee.

INGREDIENTS

100g ground almonds

100g caster sugar, split into 75g and 25g

1 orange, zest finely grated

2 egg whites

1 tbsp flaked almonds, to decorate

METHOD

Preheat the oven to Gas Mark 4 or 180°c. Line two large baking sheets with greaseproof paper or baking parchment, greased with butter to prevent the macaroons sticking.

Start by mixing the ground almonds, the 75g of caster sugar and the orange zest together in a bowl. Don't worry if the zest stays in little clumps. In another bowl, whisk the egg whites until stiff. Add the remaining 25g of caster sugar and whisk again until glossy. This is quite easy by hand with a balloon whisk, but very quick with an electric whisk.

Using a large metal spoon, fold the almond mixture gently into the whipped egg whites until well combined. Don't worry if it's slightly lumpy.

Put heaped teaspoons of the mixture onto the lined baking sheets and top each one with a few flaked almonds. They rise a little but don't spread too much during baking.

Bake the macaroons for 10 to 15 minutes until golden brown. Remove from the oven and cool on the trays before removing the macaroons from the baking parchment with a palette knife.

Dust lightly with icing sugar before serving. They keep well in an airtight container for up to 2 weeks.

GINGERBREAD BISCUITS WITH ROYAL ICING

MAKES 30

This is one of my all-time favourite biscuit recipes. Apart from tasting totally delicious, the biscuit dough is also very adaptable. Stamp out flower shapes for summer fayres, bats and pumpkins for Halloween and stars dusted with edible glitter for Christmas. We've even made a medieval fortress standing 40cm high with this recipe! This icing sets hard, so it's good to use for fine decoration on biscuits or for setting structures such as gingerbread houses.

INGREDIENTS

For the biscuits

350g plain flour

2 tsp ground ginger

1 tsp bicarbonate of soda

100g unsalted butter, diced

175g soft light brown sugar

4 tbsp golden syrup

1 egg, beaten

For the royal icing

250g icing sugar

1 egg white

1 tbsp lemon juice

1 tsp glycerine (optional)

METHOD

For the biscuits

Preheat the oven to Gas Mark 4 or 180°c. Line three large baking trays with greaseproof paper. Sieve the flour, ginger and bicarbonate of soda into a large bowl. Rub in the diced butter then stir in the sugar. Beat the syrup and egg together then tip into the dry ingredients. Stir the mixture well, gradually bringing it together with your hands. Knead for 1 or 2 minutes to form a smooth, firm ball of dough. You can refrigerate this for up to a week wrapped in greaseproof paper, but rest at room temperature before rolling out.

Roll the dough out on a floured surface until it's about 0.5cm thick, or slightly thicker if you prefer softer gingerbread. Cut out your chosen shapes and place on the lined baking trays. Bake for 10 to 20 minutes in the preheated oven, depending on the size of your gingerbread shapes and whether you like soft, chewy or crisp biscuits. They should be golden brown when done. Leave to cool slightly on the baking trays until they have hardened enough to be transferred onto a wire cooling rack using a palette knife. Once cool, the gingerbread shapes can be decorated to your liking.

For the royal icing

Sieve the icing sugar into a bowl and make a well in the centre. Lightly beat the egg white with the lemon juice then add to the icing sugar. Whisk until the icing is stiff and glossy. This takes about 10 minutes and is much easier with an electric whisk!

If you're using the icing straight away there's no need to add the glycerine; just keep the bowl covered to stop the surface drying out. If you're making a larger quantity or need time to perfect the icing, such as for a gingerbread house, then whisk the glycerine into the icing at this point, which makes it easier to work with. If you want coloured rather than white icing, just add a drop of food colouring or paste. With or without glycerine, the icing can be kept for 24 hours in a sealed pot in the fridge. Stir again before using. Once piped, leave the decorated biscuits at room temperature to set hard. This takes 10 to 15 minutes for fine, small decorations. Leave it for 24 hours to set a gingerbread house.

MOCHA BROWNIES

MAKES 25

I just had to invent a coffee and chocolate traybake; it's one of my favourite flavour combinations. These brownies are the result of my efforts: divinely rich with a well-balanced mocha flavour. I love them either plain or with nuts.

INGREDIENTS

80g unsalted butter

200g dark chocolate (70% cocoa solids)

100g soft light brown sugar

100g soft dark brown sugar

3 eggs

2 tbsp instant Americano coffee powder or 2½ tbsp freeze-dried coffee granules

2 tbsp milk

80g plain flour

100g pecans or walnuts, roughly chopped (optional)

50g dark chocolate chips or chunks

METHOD

Line the base of a 22 by 22cm baking tin with greaseproof paper and grease the sides. Preheat the oven to Gas Mark 4 or 180°c.

Start by melting the butter and chocolate together in a saucepan over a low heat or in a suitable bowl in the microwave on a low setting. Stir until completely melted.

Next, whisk the light and dark brown sugars with the eggs in a large bowl, either by hand or with an electric whisk until the mixture is pale and bubbly. Add the melted chocolate and butter to the egg mixture and gently stir together.

In a small bowl or mug, dissolve the instant coffee in the milk, warming it a little if you need to. Add it to the chocolate and egg mixture then stir briefly.

Sieve the flour into the bowl, add the nuts if you're using them, and gently stir to make sure all the ingredients are combined.

Pour the brownie mixture into the prepared baking tin, sprinkle the chocolate chips over the top and bake for 15 to 20 minutes until just set in the middle and cracked on the surface. Make sure you don't overbake them.

Remove the brownies from the oven and rest on a wire rack to cool. Cut into 25 squares to serve.

RHUBARB & HONEY MUFFINS

MAKES 12

Light and honeyed with a tang of juicy rhubarb, these muffins are perfect with a cup of refreshing green tea. The small rhubarb chunks cook perfectly within the cake mixture.

INGREDIENTS

150g fresh rhubarb

200g butter, softened

75g caster sugar

3 eggs

5 tbsp runny honey

225g self-raising flour

½ tsp baking powder

METHOD

You will need a 12-hole muffin tray and 12 paper cases. I use muffin cases or large cupcake cases. Preheat the oven to Gas Mark 4 or 180°c.

Start by chopping the rhubarb into 1cm pieces. Put to one side. In a large bowl, beat the soft butter and sugar together until creamy and light. This is easier and quicker with an electric whisk.

Add the eggs one at a time, beating after each addition. Stir in the honey. Sieve the flour and baking powder into the bowl and fold in gently with a large metal spoon. Finally, stir in the rhubarb pieces.

Fill the paper cases in the muffin tin three quarters full with the mixture, then bake in the oven for 20 minutes until the muffins are risen and golden brown.

Turn out onto a wire rack and leave until almost cool, then serve.

VERY LEMONY DRIZZLE CAKE

SERVES 6-8

This utterly delicious cake was created by my friend Sarah when she lived out in Zimbabwe with her family. She had so many juicy lemons to use up that she just had to bake cakes with them!

INGREDIENTS

2 unwaxed lemons

100g unsalted butter, softened, plus extra for greasing

175g self-raising flour

½ tsp baking powder

175g caster sugar

2 eggs

4 tbsp milk

100g icing sugar

METHOD

Preheat the oven to Gas Mark 4 or 180°c. Line the base then grease the sides of a 450g loaf tin or 22cm round cake tin.

Start by finely grating the zest from the two lemons into a small bowl. Now squeeze the juice from the lemons into a small pan. You should have about 70 to 80ml of cloudy juice. Set both aside.

Put the soft butter, flour, baking powder, caster sugar, eggs and milk into a mixing bowl. Add the lemon zest and beat well until thoroughly combined.

Pour the cake mixture into the prepared tin and bake in the preheated oven for 45 minutes or until golden brown and risen. Cool on a wire rack, but leave in the tin for now. Take a thin skewer and make a few little holes in the cake from top to bottom (this will help the lemon syrup to soak in).

Meanwhile, add the icing sugar to the lemon juice in the pan. Heat gently, stirring until the sugar is dissolved. Remove from the heat then pour the syrup slowly over the cake as it cools, making sure it soaks in evenly over the surface. There is plenty of syrup but it does all soak in!

Once the cake is completely cool and the syrup has all soaked in, remove from the tin and serve.

You can also make this into a fabulous layered celebration cake. Double the quantity and bake in two 22cm round cake tins. Once cooled, sandwich the two cakes together with whipped cream and lemon curd. You could also decorate the top with candied lemon zest. Yum!

ITALIAN-STYLE PLUM CAKE

SERVES 8-10

This most delicious of cakes is inspired by Sophie Grigson's torta di prugne. It's a large, flat Italian-style fresh fruit cake; I use our home-grown plums in the late summer which are so sweet and fruity. I've also added polenta and olive oil to give us a taste of Italy.

INGREDIENTS

600-700g ripe plums

350g plain flour

50g polenta

½ tbsp baking powder

4 eggs

250g caster sugar, plus 2 tbsp for the topping

1 tsp vanilla extract

150ml mild Italian olive oil (not extra-virgin)

METHOD

Preheat the oven to Gas Mark 4 or 180°c. Line the base of a 26cm round cake tin with greaseproof paper and grease the sides well with olive oil.

Start by halving the plums, removing the stones and cutting them into 2cm thick slices or eighths. Next, sieve the flour, polenta and baking powder together into a large bowl.

In another large bowl, whisk together the eggs, caster sugar (reserving the two tablespoons for the topping) and vanilla until the mixture is thick and pale. I use an electric whisk for about 2 minutes.

Fold half of the flour mixture into the egg and sugar mixture with a large metal spoon, followed by the olive oil and then the remaining flour mixture.

Spoon a little more than half of the cake batter into the prepared cake tin. Lay half of the plum slices evenly over the batter. Spoon the remaining cake batter over, then top with the last of the plum slices.

Sprinkle the reserved caster sugar over the top of the cake and bake for 50 to 60 minutes until golden, risen and set. Leave to cool on a wire rack before lifting out of the tin.

Serve the plum cake in large wedges dusted with icing sugar.

CINNAMON SWIRL CAKE

SERVES 6-8

This cake was inspired by a muffin recipe from the amazing Muffins Galore by Catherine Atkinson. I love the sweet cinnamon and vanilla flavour. I've included ground almonds to give the cake a more nutty texture and to make it more nutritious and filling.

INGREDIENTS

3 tsp ground cinnamon
70g soft light brown sugar
200g self-raising flour
50g ground almonds
1 tsp baking powder
100g caster sugar
Pinch of fine salt
225ml milk
1 egg
2 tsp vanilla extract
5 tbsp (75ml) vegetable oil

METHOD

Line a 19cm round cake tin with baking parchment or a ready-made fluted paper liner. Preheat the oven to Gas Mark 4 or 180°c.

Start by mixing the cinnamon and the light brown sugar in a small bowl. Make sure there are no lumps. In a large bowl, mix together the flour, ground almonds, baking powder, caster sugar and salt.

Measure the milk into a jug and add the egg, vanilla and oil to it. Lightly beat the egg into the liquids.

Add the milk mixture to the dry ingredients and stir to combine, but be careful to not overmix the cake batter as it may become dense and heavy.

Finally, tip the cinnamon sugar over the cake batter and stir just once or twice to achieve a swirl before tipping the whole lot into the prepared cake tin.

Bake for 30 to 35 minutes in the preheated oven until the cake has risen and is golden brown on top. Turn out of the tin and put on a wire rack to cool a little before serving. Watch out for the hot sugar swirl!

CHEESE SCONES

MAKES 5 LARGE OR 15-18 TINY SCONES

These are Martin's absolute favourite treat. He often makes them at the weekend and we eat them warm with salted butter. He likes to make them large, but when I make them I prefer a smaller, more dainty scone.

INGREDIENTS

250g self-raising flour

1 tbsp mustard powder (we use Colman's)

50g salted butter

120g extra mature cheddar cheese, grated

160ml semi-skimmed milk, plus 1 tbsp for brushing

METHOD

Preheat the oven to Gas Mark 7 or 210°c and lightly grease two baking trays.

Start by sieving the flour with the mustard powder into a large bowl. Add the butter, cut into small chunks, and rub into the flour with your fingertips. When the mixture resembles fine breadcrumbs, stir in the grated cheese. Add the milk and mix to a firm dough.

Turn out onto a floured work surface and roll lightly until the dough is about 2cm thick. Stamp out 9cm rounds for large scones or 4cm rounds for small scones with a cutter. Gather the excess dough together, re-roll and cut out more scones until the dough is all used up.

Place the scones on the greased baking trays, brush the tops with milk and bake in the preheated oven for about 10 minutes (less for small scones) or until risen and golden.

Cool on a wire rack before serving.

CHOCOLATE, HAZELNUT & OAT COOKIES

MAKES ABOUT 20

A classic and very yummy flavour combination that makes these cookies hard to resist. Dark chocolate chips and cocoa powder give them a rich chocolate flavour that complements the hazelnuts perfectly.

INGREDIENTS

100g unsalted butter, softened

75g light brown sugar

1 egg

3 tbsp golden syrup

75g plain flour

2 tbsp cocoa powder

½ tsp baking powder

120g porridge oats

100g dark chocolate chips or chunks

50g hazelnuts, roughly chopped

METHOD

Preheat the oven to Gas Mark 4 or 180°c. Line two large baking sheets with greaseproof paper.

Firstly, put the softened butter and sugar in a large bowl and beat together until pale and smooth.

Beat in the egg and golden syrup then sift in the flour, cocoa powder and baking powder. Mix well. Add the oats, chocolate chips and hazelnuts and stir to incorporate them. The mixture will be thick and a little sticky.

Take heaped tablespoons of the mixture and arrange the balls of cookie dough on the baking sheets, spaced a little apart. These cookies spread a little during baking.

Bake for 15 to 18 minutes until set and darker around the edges. Leave the cookies on their trays to cool and harden before lifting off the paper to serve. Store in an airtight container.

EASY ROSEMARY & SEA SALT 'FOCACCIA'

SERVES 4-6

This recipe is adapted from Darina Allen's Ballymaloe Cookery Course which is a brilliant book. It is essentially white soda bread with olive oil and Italian-style toppings. You can add olives, sliced red onion or whatever you like most. My favourite combination is fresh rosemary and sea salt.

INGREDIENTS

300g plain white flour

1 tsp bicarbonate of soda

½ tsp fine salt

300ml buttermilk or soured milk*

3 tbsp extra-virgin olive oil

4 small sprigs of fresh rosemary

½ tsp sea salt flakes

* To make soured milk, add one tablespoon of lemon juice to 300ml of cow's milk, stir and leave for 5 minutes to curdle and thicken before using.

METHOD

You'll need a small baking tray, about 22cm square. Preheat the oven to Gas Mark 8 or 220°c. Sieve the flour, bicarbonate of soda and salt into a large mixing bowl. Make a well in the centre of the flour mixture then pour all the buttermilk or soured milk and one tablespoon of the olive oil into it. Using a large wooden spoon, stir the flour into the centre from the outside in circular movements until you form a soft ball of dough.

Brush the baking tray generously with some of the remaining olive oil. Tip the dough onto the oiled tray and press it evenly into the corners. The dough can be a bit sticky at this stage so brush a little oil onto your fingertips to prevent it sticking to them. Brush the surface of the dough generously with the last of the oil then press small sprigs of rosemary at intervals into the dough. Sprinkle all over with the sea salt flakes.

Bake the 'focaccia' in the preheated oven for 15 minutes or until risen, crisp and golden on top. Take out of the oven, cool in the tray then slice into chunks for serving.

WHOLEMEAL SODA BREAD

MAKES 1 LOAF

This recipe is from the excellent baking book Bread by Eric Treuille and Ursula Ferrigno. It should be golden and crunchy on the outside and soft but close-textured inside. Using half wholemeal and half plain flour means it's not too heavy or dry. Soda bread is best eaten on the day of baking but after that it makes great toast!

INGREDIENTS

250g wholemeal flour

250g plain white flour, plus extra for dusting and kneading

1 tsp bicarbonate of soda

¼ tsp salt

25g unsalted butter

300ml buttermilk or soured milk*

* To make soured milk, add one tablespoon of lemon juice to 300ml of cow's milk, stir and leave for 5 minutes to curdle and thicken before using.

METHOD

Preheat your oven to Gas Mark 6 or 200°c. Sieve all the dry ingredients into a large bowl. Add the butter in small chunks and rub into the flour with your fingertips.

Make a well in the centre of the flour mixture and pour in the buttermilk. Stir everything together with a wooden spoon to make a soft dough. Turn out the dough onto a floured surface and knead lightly for about 3 minutes until it is smooth and elastic.

Shape the dough into a round approximately 15cm wide and 5cm thick. Dust the top with a little plain flour. Place the round on a baking tray, then with a sharp knife cut an X-shaped slash 2cm deep across the top of the loaf.

Bake the soda bread in the preheated oven for 30 to 35 minutes until golden brown. When tapped on the base it should sound hollow. Cool on a wire rack covered with a tea towel.

RUSTIC BREAD ROLLS

MAKES 8-12

This recipe originated in a book called Breadmaking by Jill Graham and is one that my mum has made in her kitchen for decades. It is one of the easiest yeasted breads that I've made, with a firm crust and a close but soft-textured inside. The second dough-rising stage takes place in the oven as it heats up to bake. I add a little wholemeal flour for flavour and fibre, and I prefer rolls, or cobs to use a Derbyshire term, as they take less time to cook than a whole loaf!

INGREDIENTS

400g strong white flour, plus extra for kneading

100g wholemeal flour

1½ tsp dried yeast (fast action or quick)

1 tsp fine salt

½ tsp caster sugar

350ml warm water

1 tbsp rapeseed oil or olive oil

METHOD

You will need a large flat baking tray, lightly greased with oil. There's no need to preheat the oven because the dough needs to prove before you will need to use it.

Start by sieving the two flours together into a warm mixing bowl. Add the yeast, salt and sugar then stir to combine. Make a well in the centre then pour the warm water and oil into the flour.

Stir the mixture to form a firm, sticky dough. Knead lightly in the bowl for 5 minutes until the dough starts to become a little more elastic.

Cover the bowl with a warm tea towel and leave in a warm, draught-free place until the dough has doubled in size. This takes about 30 to 40 minutes.

Next, turn the dough out onto a floured board or work surface. Knead again for 5 minutes until the dough is smooth and elastic, adding extra flour as needed.

Cut the ball of dough into eight to twelve equal portions, depending on how small you want them. Make each one into a round or oval shape and place them onto the greased baking tray.

Place the baking tray in the middle of the unheated oven and set the temperature to Gas Mark 5 or 190°c. The rolls will prove as the oven heats up. Bake for 15 to 20 minutes (starting from the time you placed them into the cold oven) or until the rolls are light golden brown, well risen and sound hollow when turned over and tapped on the base. Cool on a wire rack before serving.

IT'S A SOUP DAY

Soup is the best one-pan meal. Quick, easy, tasty and nourishing, it has it all. Soup can be smooth and creamy, thick and chunky, light and fragrant. You can eat it with a spoon or sip it from a mug. The thing I like most is that a soup recipe is endlessly adaptable; it appeals to my thrifty nature to use up whatever is left in the fridge.

RED PEPPER, TOMATO & BASIL SOUP

CORNBREAD

LEEK, SWEET POTATO & CHICKPEA SOUP

SPICED RED LENTIL SOUP

GREEN PEA SOUP

EASY SPRING ONION 'FOCACCIA'

SMOKED HADDOCK & SWEETCORN CHOWDER

ROAST PUMPKIN & PASTA SOUP WITH GARLIC, CHILLI & THYME

CREAMY CAULIFLOWER & GARLIC SOUP

BEETROOT SOUP

VEGETABLE STOCK

CHICKEN STOCK

RED PEPPER, TOMATO & BASIL SOUP

SERVES 6-8

I make many different variations of this soup, which is Lilia's favourite. I sometimes roast the chopped peppers and onions first to give a richer flavour. A pinch of chilli is also a tasty addition.

INGREDIENTS

4 red bell peppers

2 large red onions

2 tins of chopped tomatoes (800g)

2 tbsp double concentrate tomato puree

1 tbsp green basil pesto or 2 tbsp fresh basil leaves, chopped

1 litre vegetable or chicken stock

Pinch of caster sugar

Salt and black pepper

Fresh basil leaves, to garnish

METHOD

Simply chop the peppers and onions into rough chunks then put them into a large saucepan with all the other ingredients except the basil leaves for garnish.

Bring to the boil then simmer gently with a lid on for about 10 minutes until the vegetables are soft.

Take off the heat then puree until smooth in a liquidiser or with a handheld stick blender in the pan. Taste the soup and adjust the seasoning as needed. Serve with torn basil leaves scattered on top.

To make this into a more filling and chunky soup, add a 400g tin of drained and rinsed haricot, cannellini or butter beans and a finely chopped courgette after the blending stage. Bring to the boil for another 4 to 5 minutes to cook the courgette, then check the seasoning and serve with a generous grating of parmesan cheese.

CORNBREAD

SERVES 6

Cornbread is very nutritious and easy to make. It has a sweet and savoury flavour with an inviting texture somewhere between bread and cake.

INGREDIENTS

150g plain flour

150g polenta or fine cornmeal

2 tsp baking powder

1 tsp caster sugar

½ tsp salt

300ml milk

2 eggs, beaten

4 tbsp (60ml) vegetable oil

METHOD

Grease and line the base of a 23cm square or round baking tin. Preheat the oven to Gas Mark 6 or 200°c.

In a large bowl, combine all the dry ingredients (flour, polenta, baking powder, sugar and salt). Measure the milk into a bowl or jug, add the eggs and beat them together. Pour them over the flour and polenta mixture. Stir well to make a thick batter with no lumps. Add the oil and stir in quickly. Pour the batter into the greased and lined baking tin and put in the middle of the preheated oven.

Bake for 20 to 25 minutes until the cornbread has risen a little and is golden on top.

Cool in the tin on a wire rack before cutting into small squares or wedges to serve. This tastes delicious served with tangy cheese, turkey chilli or the red pepper, tomato and basil soup above.

LEEK, SWEET POTATO & CHICKPEA SOUP

SERVES 6

This is a wholesome, chunky soup and very easy to make. Use pre-prepared sweet potato chunks to make life even easier. The flavours of this soup work well with the addition of some cooked ham if you like.

INGREDIENTS

2-4 leeks (approx. 600g)

1 large sweet potato (approx. 700g)

1 large baking potato (approx. 400g)

250g cooked chickpeas, drained from a tin or soaked and boiled from dried

1 litre chicken or vegetable stock

2 bay leaves

Salt and black pepper

METHOD

Start by preparing the vegetables. Shred the leeks into thin, evenly-sized pieces. Peel both the potatoes and cut them into bite-size chunks, roughly 2cm square.

Next, simply put the vegetables with all the other ingredients into a large saucepan and bring to the boil, covered. Simmer gently for 15 to 20 minutes, stirring occasionally to prevent anything from sticking on the base of the pan, until the potatoes are soft and the liquid has thickened.

Taste and adjust the seasoning as needed. Serve with crusty bread.

SPICED RED LENTIL SOUP

SERVES 4-6

This soup is one of our favourites. It was originally inspired by the fabulous cook book Moro and is similar in style to a lentil dahl with gentle, warming spices. It's very simple and quick to make and very good for you too.

INGREDIENTS

1 large onion

1 stick of celery

4 fat cloves of garlic

1 tbsp vegetable oil

2 tsp cumin seeds

1 tsp ground turmeric

¼ tsp crushed red chillies (or a pinch of cayenne pepper)

300g red split lentils

1 litre vegetable or chicken stock

Pinch of sea salt

Freshly ground black pepper

1 lemon, quartered

Wholemeal pitta bread, to serve

METHOD

Start by finely chopping the onion, celery and garlic. Put the vegetable oil in a medium-size saucepan and add the chopped onion and celery.

Cook gently on a low to medium heat for 10 to 15 minutes, stirring now and then, until the onions and celery are soft but not browned. This gentle cooking gives the soup a lovely sweetness.

Once the vegetables are soft, add the garlic and spices to the pan and stir them in. Add the red lentils and stock, stir, then put a lid on the pan.

Simmer gently for 15 minutes, stirring now and then to prevent the lentils sticking to the bottom of the pan. When the lentils are completely soft, taste and season with salt and black pepper, if needed. If the soup is very thick at this stage, add some extra hot water.

Serve the soup with a squeeze of fresh lemon juice over the top and warm pitta bread on the side.

GREEN PEA SOUP &
EASY SPRING ONION 'FOCACCIA'

SERVES 4-6

This soup is so simple, tasty and green! The peas can be fresh or straight from the freezer and they are a great source of vegetable protein. The focaccia is a surprisingly delicious savoury bread, using inspiration from Lilia, who grows her own spring onions in the summer.

INGREDIENTS

For the focaccia

4 fat spring onions (about 80g)

300g plain white flour

1 tsp bicarbonate of soda

½ tsp fine salt

¼ tsp ground black pepper

300ml buttermilk or soured milk*

3 tbsp extra-virgin olive oil

½ tsp sea salt flakes

* To make soured milk, add one tablespoon of lemon juice to 300ml of cow's milk, stir and leave for 5 minutes to curdle and thicken before using.

For the soup

2 onions

2 cloves of garlic

1 tbsp vegetable oil

700g garden peas

50g spinach leaves

1 litre chicken or vegetable stock

1 tsp dried thyme or 2 sprigs of fresh thyme

Salt and black pepper

METHOD

For the focaccia

You'll need a small baking tray, about 22cm square. Preheat the oven to Gas Mark 8 or 220°c. Firstly, prepare the onions by cutting off the hard root at the base then slicing each one diagonally to give approximately 1 to 2cm slices, using the white and green parts.

Sieve the flour, bicarbonate of soda, salt and black pepper into a large mixing bowl. Make a well in the centre of the flour mixture then pour all the buttermilk or soured milk and one tablespoon of the olive oil into it, followed by the spring onion slices. Using a large wooden spoon, stir the flour into the centre from the outside in circular movements until you form a soft ball of dough.

Brush the baking tray generously with some of the remaining oil. Tip the dough onto the oiled tray and press it evenly into the corners. The dough can be a bit sticky at this stage so brush a little oil onto your fingertips to prevent it sticking. Brush the surface of the dough generously with the last of the olive oil then sprinkle all over with sea salt flakes.

Bake the 'focaccia' in the preheated oven for 15 minutes or until risen, crisp and golden on top. Take out of the oven, cool in the tray then slice into chunks.

For the soup

Start by chopping the onions and garlic. Heat the oil in a large saucepan and add the onions.

Gently cook on a low heat for 10 minutes, stirring occasionally, until the onions are soft and translucent. Then add the garlic and stir briefly.

Add the peas, spinach, stock and herbs. Cover the pan with a lid and bring to the boil.

Cook until the peas are tender, which should take about 5 to 10 minutes.

Remove the pan from the heat, take out any woody thyme sprigs and puree the soup with a handheld stick blender or liquidiser until smooth. Taste and adjust the seasoning.

Add a grind of black pepper to each bowl before serving with the focaccia.

SMOKED HADDOCK & SWEETCORN CHOWDER

SERVES 4-6

As well as a meal in one pan, this is a satisfying, tasty dish and quick to cook. Serve with crusty bread to mop up the juices. To make a creamier chowder, replace 500ml of the stock with whole milk.

INGREDIENTS

1 tbsp vegetable oil

1 medium-size leek, finely sliced

1 onion, finely sliced

1 large carrot

1 large baking potato (approx 400g)

1½ litres fish stock, or vegetable stock with 1 tbsp fish sauce

2 bay leaves

300g skinless and boneless smoked haddock

200g sweetcorn kernels (drained if tinned)

Freshly ground black pepper

Fresh chives or parsley, to garnish

METHOD

Start by heating the oil in a large saucepan, then fry the leek and onion until soft, stirring to prevent burning. Meanwhile, peel and finely dice the carrot then peel the potato and cut into bite-size pieces. Add the carrot and potato to the saucepan along with the stock and bay leaves.

Stir well, put the lid on the pan and turn up the heat. Gently boil for 10 minutes. Meanwhile, cut the haddock into bite-size chunks. Add it to the pan along with the sweetcorn and black pepper. Stir the chowder, turn the heat down a little and simmer gently for another 5 minutes until the potatoes are tender and the fish is cooked.

Taste and add salt and extra black pepper if needed. Remove the bay leaves before serving. Add a scattering of fresh chives or chopped parsley to each bowl.

ROAST PUMPKIN & PASTA SOUP WITH GARLIC, CHILLI & THYME

SERVES 6-8

A soup for cold weather, this has a thick, smooth texture with small pasta pieces to add bite. Plenty of garlic and a good kick of chilli add to its warming flavour.

INGREDIENTS

1kg pumpkin or squash, in chunks (prepared weight)

1 tbsp vegetable oil

4 carrots

1 stick of celery

1 onion

6 cloves of garlic

1 tsp red chilli flakes

3 sprigs of fresh thyme or 1½ tsp dried thyme

1 litre chicken or vegetable stock

Salt and black pepper

100g mini pasta shapes, orzo or spaghetti broken into 1-2cm lengths

Soured cream, to garnish

METHOD

Preheat the oven to Gas Mark 6 or 200°c. Start by preparing the pumpkin or squash. Chop, peel and remove the seeds. Cut the flesh into large chunks (about 4 to 6cm square). Put them into a roasting tray and drizzle with the oil. Roast the pumpkin or squash in the preheated oven for 20 to 30 minutes until soft and tinged with brown.

Next, prepare all the other vegetables. Peel and roughly chop the carrots, celery, onion and garlic, then put everything into a large saucepan with the chilli, thyme and stock.

Bring to the boil, cover and simmer for 15 minutes or until the vegetables are soft. Once the pumpkin or squash has cooked, remove from the oven and carefully transfer into the saucepan.

Remove the thyme sprigs (if you used fresh) then liquidise or blend the soup until smooth. Taste and add salt or pepper if needed.

Finally, add the pasta to the soup with a little more water if it's very thick, then put the pan back on the heat and bring to the boil, stirring occasionally, until the pasta has cooked.

Serve with a swirl of soured cream in each bowl.

CREAMY CAULIFLOWER & GARLIC SOUP

SERVES 4-6

This soup has a light, almost whipped, creamy texture. It is quick and easy to make. Garlic-infused oil is a lovely addition if you have some.

INGREDIENTS

25g butter

1 onion, chopped

6-8 cloves of garlic, sliced

1 cauliflower (approx. 600g) broken into florets and roughly chopped

500ml chicken or vegetable stock

150ml single cream

Salt and black pepper

Garlic-infused oil (optional)

Flat leaf parsley, to garnish

METHOD

Melt the butter in a large saucepan. Add the chopped onion and fry gently on a low heat for about 5 minutes until soft but not browned.

Add the garlic and fry gently for another minute then add the cauliflower florets and stir to coat with the butter.

Next, add the stock to the pan, cover with a lid and bring to a slow boil. Cook for 5 to 10 minutes. Once the cauliflower is tender, remove the pan from the heat, add the cream and then blend well until smooth, creamy and frothy using a handheld stick blender or liquidiser.

Taste the soup, adding salt and black pepper if required. Finish with the garlic oil and a sprinkle of finely chopped parsley.

BEETROOT SOUP

SERVES 4-6

The colour of this soup is rich and vibrant, the flavour earthy and warming. Serve with hot buttered toast on a cold day.

INGREDIENTS

800-900g raw beetroot

1 tbsp vegetable oil

1 onion

2 cloves of garlic

1 litre chicken or vegetable stock

1 tsp sage (dried or fresh and chopped)

100ml single cream, plus extra to serve

Salt and black pepper

METHOD

Firstly, put the beetroot into a large pan of water, bring to the boil and cook until tender. Drain and leave to cool.

In the meantime, heat the oil in a large saucepan, chop the onion and garlic and fry on a low heat until soft but not browned.

Once the beetroot is cool enough to handle, using gloves to protect your hands from staining, gently rub off the thin outer skin. Chop off any hard stems or roots then cut into chunks.

Add the beetroot chunks to the onions with the stock and sage. Put a lid on the pan then bring to a slow boil for a few minutes.

Puree the soup with a handheld stick blender or liquidiser until smooth, then add the cream and stir into the soup. Taste and check the seasoning, adding salt and pepper as needed.

Serve warm with an extra swirl of cream on top of each bowl.

VEGETABLE STOCK

MAKES APPROX. 1½ LITRES

A light, tasty stock to enhance soups, rice dishes and sauces.

INGREDIENTS

1 onion

1 carrot

1 stick of celery

1 tsp whole black peppercorns

2 large bay leaves

2 sprigs of fresh parsley

2 sprigs of fresh thyme

125ml white wine (optional)

1½ litres water (use reserved vegetable cooking water if you can)

METHOD

Roughly chop the onion, carrot and celery then put them in a large pan with all the other ingredients. Bring to the boil then cover with a lid and simmer for 1 hour.

Skim the surface with a large spoon to remove any scum that forms. Strain the stock through a sieve to remove all the vegetables, peppercorns and herbs.

Let it cool, then cover and refrigerate if not using immediately. Freeze in portions to keep for longer.

CHICKEN STOCK

MAKES ABOUT 1½ LITRES

A good stock is the basis of a great-tasting soup. Chicken stock is also particularly nutritious. It freezes well too.

INGREDIENTS

800g chicken bones or the carcass from a roast chicken

1 small onion

1 carrot

1 stick of celery

1 tsp whole black peppercorns

2 large bay leaves

1 sprig of sage

125ml white wine (optional)

1½ litres water

METHOD

Put the chicken bones or carcass into a large saucepan. Roughly chop the onion, carrot and celery then add to the pan with all the other ingredients.

Bring to the boil then cover the pan with a lid and simmer for about 2 hours. Skim the surface with a large spoon to remove any scum that forms.

Strain the stock through a sieve to remove all the bones, vegetables and herbs. Let it cool then cover and refrigerate for up to 3 days or use as required. Freeze in portions to keep for longer.

OUTSIDE...
SALADS & PICNICS

When the weather's warm we love to eat outside in the garden, sometimes light the barbecue
or take a picnic further afield. This is food for warm summer days and long,
balmy evenings.

SAVOURY TURKEY ROLLS

RAINBOW COLESLAW

TUNA & TOMATO PASTIES

GREEK-STYLE CHEESE PIE

ROAST SWEET PEPPER & CHERRY TOMATO SALSA

SMOKED MACKEREL PÂTÉ

POACHED CHICKEN WITH GREEN LENTILS,
WATERCRESS & MUSTARD DRESSING

BABY POTATO, SMOKED MACKEREL & TOMATO SALAD

WHITE BEAN SALAD WITH
ROSEMARY & GARLIC DRESSING

BEETROOT, GOAT'S CHEESE & ORANGE SALAD

YOGHURT & CUCUMBER DIP WITH GARLIC & DILL

LEAFY GREEN SALAD WITH VINAIGRETTE DRESSING

PICKLED SUMMER VEGETABLES

LEMON ICED TEA

SAVOURY TURKEY ROLLS & RAINBOW COLESLAW

SERVES 8-10

These pastry rolls are delicious eaten warm or cold with salad and potatoes, perfect for a picnic.

INGREDIENTS

For the rolls

750g turkey thigh and breast mince

150g mature cheddar cheese

1 egg

1 small onion, finely chopped

3 cloves of garlic, finely chopped

3 tbsp double concentrate tomato puree

2 tsp finely chopped fresh sage leaves or ½ tsp dried sage

½ tsp red chilli flakes or ¼ tsp hot chilli powder

1 tsp fennel seeds

½ tsp fine sea salt

Freshly ground black pepper

500g shortcrust pastry

Plain flour, for dusting and rolling

3 tbsp milk, for glazing

For the coleslaw

300-350g white, red or mixed cabbage

1 small courgette (approx. 150g)

1 medium carrot (approx. 100g)

3-5 radishes (approx. 50g)

1 small red onion or 2-3 spring onions (approx. 50g)

1 small red or green apple

2-3 tbsp fresh green herbs (parsley, basil, chives, lemon balm)

2 tbsp cider vinegar

5 tbsp (75ml) rapeseed or olive oil

Large pinch of caster sugar and salt

METHOD

For the rolls

You will need one large, flat baking tray. Preheat the oven to Gas Mark 6 or 200°c.

Start by grating the chesse and putting all the filling ingredients (everything except the pastry, flour and milk) into a large bowl, then mix until thoroughly combined.

Roll out the pastry on a floured surface to make two oblong sheets (about 32 by 22cm each or to fit the length of your baking tray).

Transfer the pastry sheets, one at a time, onto the baking tray then divide the turkey filling between them, moulding it into shape along the length to make two long rolls.

Fold the pastry over to completely cover the filling, sealing the long edge with a dab of milk, but keeping the short ends open. Carefully flip over each roll so that the pastry seam is underneath.

Brush the tops of the pastry rolls with milk then bake in the preheated oven for 30 to 40 minutes until firm and golden. Leave to cool before transferring to a plate or board. Cut into slices to serve.

For the coleslaw

Simply wash and prepare then grate or finely slice all the vegetables and the apple into a large bowl.

Chop the fresh herbs, add them to the bowl and stir everything together.

In a small jug or bowl, whisk the vinegar and oil together with the sugar and salt. Taste and adjust the seasoning before adding the dressing to the vegetables. Toss well then refrigerate until needed.

TUNA & TOMATO PASTIES

MAKES 8

A very tasty picnic food and a good alternative to sandwiches. I sometimes add a few chopped green olives or capers to the filling for a salty burst of flavour. If you need to save time, use ready-made shortcrust pastry. The filling can be made in advance and stored for several days in the fridge.

INGREDIENTS

For the pastry
125g plain flour

125g wholemeal flour

Pinch of sea salt

125g unsalted butter, chilled

1 egg

1 tbsp milk, for glazing

For the filling
1 tbsp vegetable oil

1 large onion, finely chopped

1 large clove of garlic, crushed or finely chopped

200g tuna chunks or flakes (drained weight from tinned tuna in spring water)

1 ripe tomato, finely chopped

2 tbsp double concentrate tomato puree

1 tsp dried oregano

Pinch of sea salt

Freshly ground black pepper

METHOD

You will need two large baking trays. Preheat the oven to Gas Mark 6 or 200°c.

For the pastry

Mix the two flours together in a large bowl with the salt. Add the cold butter in small chunks and rub into the flour with the tips of your fingers until the mixture resembles fine breadcrumbs.

In a small bowl or mug, beat the egg lightly with a teaspoon of cold water and add it to the flour mixture. Gently stir them together until a ball of dough is formed, adding a drop more cold water if needed. Leave the pastry in the bowl covered with a clean tea towel while you make the filling.

For the filling

Heat the oil in a frying pan then add the chopped onion and garlic. Cook on a medium heat for 5 minutes, stirring now and then, until the onion is soft. Then add the drained tuna, chopped tomato including all the seeds and juice, tomato puree, oregano, salt and black pepper. Stir well to combine everything and soften the tomatoes, then remove the pan from the heat and let it cool.

Roll out the pastry on a floured surface until it's about 0.5cm thick. Use a small plate or saucer about 15.5 cm (6 inches) in diameter as a template; place it upside down on the pastry and cut around the edge with a knife. Gather and re-roll the pastry until it's all used up and you have eight circles. Lightly grease the baking trays.

Divide the tuna and tomato filling into eight equal portions. Working with one at a time, brush milk around the outer edge of the pastry circle, spoon a portion of filling into the centre then fold the pastry in half and gently crimp the curved edge between two fingers to seal the pasty.

When you have done all eight, brush the tops of the pasties with a little more milk and place them onto the greased baking trays. Bake in the preheated oven for 25 to 30 minutes until golden, then remove and cool on a wire rack. Serve at room temperature with salad or as part of a picnic.

GREEK-STYLE CHEESE PIE WITH ROAST SWEET PEPPER & CHERRY TOMATO SALSA

SERVES 4-6

We've enjoyed cheese pies similar to this on holiday in Greece; it always makes me think of summertime. The flavours of the herbs lend a subtle balance to the rich cheeses, and the filo pastry provides a crisp but flaky outer shell. The salsa is a vibrant accompaniment which also goes well with grilled or barbecued food.

INGREDIENTS

For the pie

2 eggs

200g feta cheese, crumbled

200g full-fat soft cheese or cream cheese

250g ricotta

25g (5-6 tbsp) chives or the green parts from 2-3 spring onions, finely chopped

3 tbsp finely chopped flat leaf parsley

Freshly ground black pepper

4 tbsp rapeseed or olive oil

100-150g (4-6 sheets) filo pastry

For the salsa

3 red and yellow bell peppers

Vegetable oil

250g cherry or baby plum tomatoes (use different varieties for colour)

½ a small red onion, finely chopped

1 clove of garlic, finely chopped

½ tsp crushed red chillies

½ tsp caster sugar

½ tbsp balsamic vinegar

1 tbsp cold-pressed rapeseed oil or extra-virgin olive oil

Pinch of sea salt flakes

Large handful of fresh basil leaves, roughly torn

METHOD

For the pie

You will need a 20cm square or round ovenproof baking tin, at least 5cm deep. Preheat the oven to Gas Mark 5 or 190°c. Start by making the filling. Put the eggs, cheeses, chives or spring onions, parsley and seasoning into a bowl. Mix together into a lumpy paste.

Take the baking tin and brush the insides well with oil. Reserve one sheet of filo pastry for the top of the pie. Put the next sheet of filo into the tin, overlapping the sides, and brush the pastry with oil. Place another sheet of filo on top of the first, again overlapping the edges, and brush with oil. Repeat with the remaining filo sheets until you have covered the inside of the tin completely and made a 'shell' for the filling.

Spoon the cheese mixture into the pastry shell and then cover the top layer by layer with the overhanging filo sheets, like wrapping a parcel, brushing with oil as you go. Finish by layering over the reserved filo sheet, folding and 'scrunching' as needed to form a lid for the pie. Brush the top thoroughly with oil.

Bake the pie in the preheated oven for 25 to 30 minutes until golden brown and crispy on the outside and set in the middle. Serve warm in squares or wedges.

For the salsa

Preheat the oven to Gas Mark 4 or 180°c. Start by washing and cutting the peppers into quarters. Put the peppers in a roasting tin, drizzle with a small amount of oil and roast in the preheated oven until soft and slightly charred at the edges. This takes about 30 minutes.

Meanwhile, chop all the little tomatoes in half (a little tedious but worth the effort) and put them into a medium-size bowl. In a small bowl, combine the finely chopped onion and garlic with the chillies, sugar, balsamic vinegar, oil and salt. Pour this mixture over the tomatoes and stir well to combine.

When the peppers are done, take them out of the oven and leave until they are cool enough to handle. Roughly chop each quarter into six or seven smaller pieces and add them to the tomato mixture. Stir the salsa to combine the flavours, adding any juices from the roasting tin.

Scatter the basil leaves over the salsa and gently mix through. Serve at room temperature.

SMOKED MACKEREL PÂTÉ

SERVES 6

Amelia especially loves this, and the recipe is so easy that she learned to make it when she was quite small. It's packed with flavour and goodness and keeps well in the fridge.

INGREDIENTS

200g smoked mackerel fillets

250g ricotta or quark (plain soft cheese)

25g unsalted butter, softened

2 tbsp horseradish sauce

Freshly ground black pepper, to taste

METHOD

Firstly, remove the skin and any bones from the mackerel fillets. Roughly break up the fish into a medium-size bowl and add all the other ingredients.

Blend the mixture with a handheld stick blender until you have a smooth, soft paste. Taste for seasoning then transfer into a serving bowl.

Keep the pâté covered and chilled until ready to use. Serve with lemon wedges, crisp breads, carrot, cucumber and radishes for dipping.

POACHED CHICKEN WITH GREEN LENTILS, WATERCRESS & MUSTARD DRESSING

SERVES 4-6

This is a great meal for sharing, served in a large dish in the middle of the table for everyone to help themselves. Double the quantities if you have a crowd. It's also a dish that can be prepared in advance as the separate components keep well in the fridge.

INGREDIENTS

For the poached chicken

1 medium-size free-range chicken or 1 large chicken crown

½ a glass of white wine

1 bay leaf

1 carrot, sliced

1 onion, sliced

½ tsp whole black peppercorns

For the lentil salad & mustard dressing

250g green lentils

1 small red onion

2 tsp wholegrain mustard

2 tbsp white wine vinegar

½ tsp sugar

Pinch of salt

6 tbsp cold-pressed rapeseed oil

Freshly ground black pepper

100g watercress

METHOD

For the poached chicken

Put all the ingredients into a large lidded saucepan or stock pot along with just enough water to cover the chicken. Bring to a simmer and cook gently for up to 1 hour until the chicken is well done and the juices run clear.

Let the chicken cool in the poaching broth then transfer it to a serving dish in the fridge until needed. Strain the broth with a sieve and reserve the liquid to use in the lentil salad below.

For the lentil salad & mustard dressing

Start by rinsing the green lentils in a sieve under the cold tap then put them in a saucepan with 1 litre of the reserved poaching broth. Bring to the boil and simmer for 15 to 20 minutes, until the lentils are tender but not mushy. Drain and place in a serving bowl to cool. Finely slice the red onion and mix into the lentils.

In a small bowl or jug, whisk together the mustard, vinegar, sugar and salt until well combined. Add the oil slowly, whisking well until the mixture has thickened. Taste and add more sugar or salt if needed along with a grind of black pepper.

To serve

Mix half of the mustard dressing into the lentil and onion salad then arrange the watercress on top. Slice the chicken into manageable pieces and place on top of the salad, finishing with a drizzle of the remaining dressing.

BABY POTATO, SMOKED MACKEREL & TOMATO SALAD

SERVES 4-6

This meal is such a favourite of ours. I serve it mostly in spring and summer, chilled with crisp green leaves. However, on cooler days I serve the potatoes and beans warm, drizzled with the lemony dressing, in one bowl and the mackerel, tomatoes and spring onions in another, with crusty bread on the side. One salad, two ways!

INGREDIENTS

750g baby waxy new potatoes

100g fine green beans (fresh or frozen)

300-400g smoked mackerel fillets

5 ripe salad tomatoes

2 spring onions

1 lemon, juiced

3 tbsp cold-pressed rapeseed oil

2 tbsp chopped flat leaf parsley

1 tbsp chopped chives

Freshly ground black pepper

METHOD

Start by bringing a large pan of water to the boil. Cook the baby potatoes whole in the boiling water until tender.

Meanwhile, trim the stalks off the tops of the green beans and then halve them to get bite-size pieces approximately 5cm long. Add the beans to the boiling water right at the end of the cooking time until just done but with a crunch, as you don't want soggy, limp beans.

Plunge the cooked potatoes and beans into cold water for a few minutes, then drain well and transfer into a serving bowl.

Remove the skins and any obvious bones from the mackerel fillets then break them into chunky pieces and add to the serving bowl.

Chop the tomatoes into bite-size pieces then finely slice the spring onions. Add them to the serving bowl on top of the potatoes and mackerel.

Mix together the lemon juice, rapeseed oil, parsley and chives in a small bowl or mug. Drizzle this dressing over the salad ingredients and toss to coat everything. Add a little black pepper if you like.

Refrigerate the dressed salad until ready to eat. Serve with crisp green leaves and lemon wedges.

WHITE BEAN SALAD
WITH ROSEMARY & GARLIC DRESSING

SERVES 4-6

This is an easy Mediterranean-style dish which is delicious eaten simply with focaccia or ciabatta bread to mop up the dressing. Alternatively, serve it with grilled chicken, fish or cold meats and cheeses as part of a larger meal.

INGREDIENTS

5 tbsp (75ml) extra-virgin olive oil

1 tbsp finely chopped fresh rosemary

1 clove of garlic, finely chopped

500-550g cooked white beans (I use a mixture of haricot, cannellini and borlotti beans)

2 large ripe tomatoes, finely diced

½ tsp salt

½ tsp caster sugar

1 tbsp white wine vinegar

50g rocket leaves

METHOD

In a small saucepan, gently warm the olive oil with the rosemary and garlic. Take off the heat, cover and leave to cool and infuse.

If you're using dried beans, you'll need to soak them overnight then cook them according to the packet instructions before use. If you have tinned beans, just drain and rinse them thoroughly.

Transfer the prepared beans to a serving bowl. Put the finely diced tomatoes into a small bowl and add the salt, sugar, vinegar and the cooled olive oil with all the rosemary and garlic. Pour the dressing over the beans and gently stir to combine. Taste and adjust the seasoning if needed.

Serve at room temperature with the rocket leaves piled on top.

BEETROOT, GOAT'S CHEESE & ORANGE SALAD

SERVES 4

This classic flavour combination of earthy beetroot, tangy cheese and fruity orange also looks beautiful on a plate. The red onion becomes mild and savoury in the dressing and brings all the flavours together. Oregano grows in abundance in our garden and is rich in antioxidants. The leaves and flowers are a pretty addition to the salad. It works equally well without the goat's cheese too.

INGREDIENTS

4 medium-size raw beetroot (approx. 350-400g) or cooked vacuum-packed beetroot

2-3 oranges

1 small red onion (approx. 50g)

300g Crottin de Chavignol or soft-ripened goat's cheese

1 tbsp rapeseed or olive oil

2 tbsp cider vinegar

Pinch of salt

2-3 tbsp fresh oregano leaves or ½ tsp dried oregano

2 tbsp fresh thyme leaves

2 tbsp fresh chopped parsley

METHOD

Firstly, bring a saucepan full of water to the boil, add the beetroot (if using raw) and cook until tender. Drain and set aside to cool.

Pare the zest from half of one of the oranges, put this into a small bowl and set aside. Thinly slice the red onion and add it to the orange zest.

With a sharp knife, peel the oranges over a plate, remove any hard pith and cut the segments into bite-size pieces. Pour all the juice that escapes over the red onion and orange zest.

Once the beetroot is cool enough to handle, using gloves to protect your hands from staining, gently rub off the outer skin. Chop off any hard stems or roots then cut into small bite-size wedges.

Cut the goat's cheese into similar size wedges then arrange it with the beetroot and orange pieces in a serving bowl.

Finally, add the oil, vinegar, salt and herbs to the red onion and zest mixture. Stir well, taste to check the seasoning then spoon the dressing over the salad in the serving bowl.

YOGHURT & CUCUMBER DIP
WITH GARLIC & DILL

SERVES 4-6

I love the combination of garlic and dill in this fresh-tasting dip. It's great with salads, grilled meats and fish. Best if made and eaten on the same day.

INGREDIENTS

400g thick, full-fat plain yoghurt

½ a large cucumber (approx. 150g)

1 clove of garlic

1 tbsp finely chopped fresh dill

Pinch of fine salt

Drizzle of extra-virgin olive oil, to serve

METHOD

Put the yoghurt into a serving bowl. Coarsely grate the cucumber (no need to peel it) and finely chop the garlic. Simply stir all the ingredients into the yoghurt, drizzle with olive oil and serve.

LEAFY GREEN SALAD
WITH VINAIGRETTE DRESSING

SERVES 4-6 AS AN ACCOMPANIMENT

A freshly made dressing on a green salad is the perfect accompaniment to many dishes. Dressings keep well in the fridge, so I often make double the quantity to store in a table-worthy slim glass bottle. A herb infused oil or vinegar is a tasty addition if you have it, as is a sliver or two of fresh garlic. My favourite herbs for this dressing are tarragon or chives.

INGREDIENTS

100-120g mixed fresh salad leaves and soft herbs, washed and spun to remove all water

2 tsp Dijon or mild smooth mustard

1 tsp fine salt

2 tsp caster sugar

2 tbsp white wine vinegar

6 tbsp extra-virgin olive or cold-pressed rapeseed oil

1 tbsp fresh herbs, chopped (optional)

METHOD

Mix the mustard, salt, sugar and vinegar together in a jug or bowl until smooth. Slowly add the oil, whisking or stirring quickly to combine. The dressing should thicken when whisked.

Add the chopped herbs and stir, then serve the dressing over the green salad leaves. Any leftover dressing can be refrigerated for up to a week. Shake well before using.

PICKLED SUMMER VEGETABLES

MAKES ENOUGH TO FILL A 1 LITRE JAR

This is an easy and tasty way to pickle vegetables for eating in salads, sandwiches or serving with barbecued food. The pickling liquid is sweet and fragrant and lasts in the fridge for weeks, the flavours mellow over time and brightly coloured vegetables can turn the liquid a pretty pink or orange. Pickled foods are traditionally used to aid the digestion.

INGREDIENTS

1 tsp coriander seeds

½ tsp fennel seeds

200ml warm water

6 tbsp caster sugar

1 tsp fine salt

300ml cider vinegar

2 bay leaves

½ unwaxed orange, zested

400g fresh vegetables (such as radishes, fennel, red onion, carrots)

METHOD

You will need a 750ml to 1 litre wide-necked glass jar with a lid, a Kilner jar or several smaller jam jars, thoroughly washed and dried.

Firstly, toast the coriander and fennel seeds in a dry saucepan for 1 to 2 minutes over a low heat. Carefully add the water, sugar and salt to the pan and stir to dissolve.

Add the vinegar, bay leaves and orange zest. Bring the pickling liquid to the boil then take the pan off the heat and allow it to cool a little.

Meanwhile, wash then prepare and thinly slice the vegetables, making sure they are free of blemishes. A mandoline helps here if you have one.

Fill your clean and dry jar with the sliced vegetables then pour the pickling liquid over them. Put the lid on tightly and allow to cool completely before labelling and storing in the fridge until needed.

LEMON ICED TEA

MAKES 1½ LITRES

This drink is so very refreshing on a hot day. You can make it stronger or sweeter to your taste. Decorate with lemon verbena leaves and lemon slices.

INGREDIENTS

3 tea bags or 2 tbsp loose black tea leaves

1½ litres hot water, just boiled

5-6 tbsp caster sugar

2 unwaxed lemons

Ice cubes

Lemon verbena or mint, to garnish

METHOD

Place the tea bags or tea leaves (in an infuser) into a large jug or bowl, pour over the hot water, cover and leave to infuse and cool, stirring now and then, for about 1 hour.

Remove the tea bags or infuser then stir in the sugar. Add the juice from one of the lemons and taste for sweetness, adding more sugar if needed.

Slice the remaining lemon and add to the tea. Refrigerate until ready to serve. Remove the lemon slices after 8 hours if any tea is left, as the flavour from the rinds can become too bitter.

Serve in tall glasses, half-filled with ice cubes and garnished with little sprigs of lemon verbena or mint.

PERFECT PASTA

Well cooked pasta with a mouth-watering sauce is one of life's most delicious meals, in my opinion! These recipes include as many Italian-style ingredients as possible. I love to use good olive oil, fresh rosemary, sage, basil and flat leaf parsley from my garden with fennel, garlic or chilli to capture that Italian essence. I usually add a pinch of sugar to tomato sauces which enhances the sun-ripened sweetness that I've only ever tasted in sunny climates.

LINGUINE WITH AUBERGINE
& SUN-DRIED TOMATO SAUCE

CONCHIGLIE WITH VEGETABLE & LENTIL RAGU

HOMEMADE TOMATO SAUCE FOR PASTA

BEEF RAGU WITH GNOCCHI

SPAGHETTI WITH SARDINES, FENNEL & LEMON

SPIRALI WITH BUTTERNUT SQUASH,
GORGONZOLA & SAGE

TAGLIATELLE WITH SMOKED SALMON,
CREME FRAICHE & GREEN VEGETABLES

BROCCOLI, RICOTTA & TOMATO PASTA SALAD

PASTA & BEAN SALAD WITH LEMON & MINT DRESSING

LINGUINE WITH AUBERGINE & SUN-DRIED TOMATO SAUCE

SERVES 4-6

This is one of my favourite pasta sauces. The aubergine and olive oil lend a velvety texture to the sauce while the garlic and sun-dried tomatoes add depth of flavour.

INGREDIENTS

1 stick of celery, finely sliced

1 red onion, finely sliced

3 tbsp olive oil

1 large or two small aubergines (approx. 500g)

4 cloves of garlic, finely sliced

1 tsp dried oregano

500g passata

100g sun-dried tomatoes, chopped (keep any oil from the jar to cook with)

½ tsp sugar

Salt and freshly ground black pepper

400g linguine

Parmesan

Fresh basil

METHOD

You'll need a large frying pan and a large saucepan with a lid. Start by gently frying the finely sliced celery and onion in the olive oil for 10 minutes until soft but not browned. If the sun-dried tomatoes were preserved in a flavoursome oil, you can use that here too. Meanwhile, chop the aubergine into very small cubes.

Add the aubergine, garlic and oregano to the pan. Stir well and cook gently for a further 5 minutes until the aubergine starts to soften.

Add the tomato passata, sun-dried tomatoes and sugar to the vegetables. Stir briefly then turn up the heat a little to simmer gently for about 20 to 30 minutes with the lid on.

Stir occasionally to prevent sticking and add a splash of water if the sauce becomes too thick. The aubergine should be fully cooked and soft after this time.

Meanwhile, bring a large saucepan of water to the boil. Add a pinch of salt then the linguine. Cook until al dente which means cooked but slightly firm to bite, then drain and transfer to a serving dish.

Taste the sauce and add salt and black pepper as needed, then serve it over the linguine with shavings of parmesan cheese and freshly torn basil leaves on top.

CONCHIGLIE WITH VEGETABLE & LENTIL RAGU

SERVES 6

This rich vegetable and lentil sauce lends itself well to coating pasta shells. Infused with rosemary and thyme, it's perfect with a generous topping of grated parmesan cheese.

INGREDIENTS

2 tbsp vegetable oil

1 large carrot, finely diced

1 stick of celery, finely sliced

1 large onion, finely chopped

3 cloves of garlic, finely chopped or minced

2 tins of chopped tomatoes (800g)

300g cooked green lentils

2 tsp fresh rosemary, chopped

1 tsp fresh thyme leaves

½ tsp soft brown sugar

Pinch of sea salt

Freshly ground black pepper

400g conchiglie (pasta shells)

Parmesan, finely grated

METHOD

Start by heating the oil in a large saucepan. Add the prepared carrot, celery and onion. Cook on a low heat for 15 minutes, stirring occasionally until soft.

Add the garlic, tomatoes, lentils, herbs, sugar, salt and pepper. Stir well, then simmer uncovered for about 10 minutes until the mixture has thickened and the vegetables are soft.

Meanwhile, bring a large pan of water to the boil, add a pinch of salt then tip in the conchiglie and cook until al dente. Drain well then tip into a warmed serving bowl.

Top the conchiglie with the vegetable ragu and grated parmesan to serve.

HOMEMADE TOMATO SAUCE FOR PASTA

MAKES ABOUT 1.4KG

This sauce is so tasty and versatile. Great if you have a glut of tomatoes to use up in the summer and perfect for freezing in batches. It takes time on the hob to slowly cook and release the flavours, leaving you free to prepare the pasta, or just sit with a glass of wine enjoying the aromas!

INGREDIENTS

3 tbsp olive oil

2 onions, finely chopped

2 carrots, finely chopped

1 stick of celery, finely chopped

2 cloves of garlic, finely chopped

3 tins of chopped tomatoes or 1.2kg fresh chopped tomatoes

2 tbsp finely chopped fresh rosemary

2 tbsp finely chopped fresh sage

2 tbsp finely chopped flat leaf parsley

2 tbsp double concentrate tomato puree

2 tsp caster sugar

Pinch of salt

Freshly ground black pepper

METHOD

Start by heating the oil in a large saucepan. Add the finely chopped onions, carrots and celery. Cook on a low heat for 20 to 30 minutes until soft but not browned.

Add the garlic and tomatoes, chopped herbs, tomato puree, sugar, salt and pepper. Put a lid on the saucepan, turn up the heat and gently simmer for 30 to 40 minutes, stirring occasionally.

The sauce will become thicker and fragrant. Taste it, then add more salt and pepper if needed. When you're happy with the flavour and consistency, take the pan off the heat. If you prefer a smoother texture, blend the sauce at this stage with a handheld stick blender or liquidiser.

Freeze the sauce in portions for another day, or serve as it is, over pasta with a grating of cheese. You could also add fish, meatballs or mixed cooked beans for variety.

BEEF RAGU WITH GNOCCHI

SERVES 4-6

This rich ragu enhanced with red wine, mushrooms and rosemary is delicious with the little soft and sticky potato dumplings called gnocchi. This ragu is also perfect as part of a baked, or al forno, dish. Layer it over cooked pasta and top with a creamy bechamel and plenty of grated parmesan cheese. A real treat!

INGREDIENTS

2 tbsp olive oil

1 onion, finely chopped

1 stick of celery, finely chopped

150g smoked lardons or streaky bacon, cubed

125ml full-bodied red wine

2 cloves of garlic, finely sliced

1 tsp salt

1 tbsp chopped fresh rosemary

200g mushrooms, finely sliced

300-400g minced beef

500g passata

½ tsp sugar

500g potato gnocchi

Salt and black pepper

Parmesan, finely grated

METHOD

Heat the olive oil in a large saucepan or frying pan, then add the finely chopped onion, celery and lardons. Cook for 5 to 10 minutes on a medium heat to gently brown all the ingredients.

Add the red wine and stir, then wait for most of the wine to evaporate before adding the garlic, salt, rosemary and mushrooms. Cook for 5 minutes or until the mushrooms are soft.

Add the beef to the pan, stir and cook until browned then add the tomato passata and sugar. Stir well and bring to a gentle simmer for 5 to 10 minutes until thick and rich.

Meanwhile, bring a saucepan of water to the boil. Add the gnocchi and boil until they rise to the surface. This takes only a few minutes. Drain the gnocchi and transfer them into a serving dish.

Taste the sauce, adding salt and black pepper as needed.

Pour the ragu over the gnocchi, grate the parmesan and serve with a crisp green salad dressed with a drizzle of olive oil and balsamic vinegar, or lightly steamed green beans.

SPAGHETTI WITH SARDINES, FENNEL & LEMON

SERVES 4-6

This is a classic Sicilian dish using the best seasonal ingredients. It is ideally served with long pasta such as spaghetti or linguine. The complex flavours combine to make a very tasty, satisfying dish. I sometimes make it with mackerel, which is just as tasty.

INGREDIENTS

1 large fennel bulb (approx. 350g)

4 tbsp olive oil

3 cloves of garlic, finely sliced

¼ tsp crushed red chilli flakes

1 tsp fennel seeds

125ml dry white wine

2 tbsp raisins

1 large lemon, zested and juiced

125ml water

4 x 120g tins of sardines in olive oil or 400g fresh sardine fillets

100g pine nuts

400g spaghetti or linguine

Salt and black pepper

METHOD

Start by finely slicing the fennel, reserving the green 'frondy' tops for garnishing. Heat the olive oil in a large pan. Add the fennel and cook gently for 15 to 20 minutes until it is soft and golden.

Add the finely sliced garlic, chilli flakes, fennel seeds, white wine, raisins, lemon zest and water to the pan. Stir and continue to cook gently for 1 to 2 minutes until the liquid has reduced.

Now add the sardines with their oil, the lemon juice and the pine nuts. Stir to combine and cook for another 2 minutes on a low heat.

Meanwhile, bring a large pan of water to the boil, add a pinch of salt then the spaghetti and cook until al dente.

Taste the sardine sauce and add salt and pepper as needed. Drain the spaghetti then serve the sauce over it with wedges of fresh lemon and the reserved fennel tops as a garnish.

SPIRALI WITH BUTTERNUT SQUASH, GORGONZOLA & SAGE

SERVES 4-6

Tangy, creamy gorgonzola cheese melts over the sweet butternut squash with the punchy garlic and fragrant sage. A real treat for your taste buds. Short pasta spirals are great with this sauce. I like to serve a crisp green salad with this dish.

INGREDIENTS

1 small butternut squash or approx. 500g pre-prepared chunks

400g spirali (pasta spirals)

1 tbsp olive oil

1 onion, thinly sliced

3 cloves of garlic, finely chopped

2 tbsp chopped fresh sage leaves or 2 tsp dried sage

250g gorgonzola cheese, cubed

100ml single cream

Freshly ground black pepper

METHOD

You'll need a large saucepan with a steamer and lid, and a large frying pan. First, carefully prepare the butternut squash with a sharp knife. Chop in half lengthways and remove the seeds with a spoon, then peel. Finally, cut it into bite-size chunks.

Bring a large pan of water to the boil and add a pinch of salt. Add the pasta to the boiling water and put the butternut squash in the steamer over the top. Remove the squash when it's tender and tip into a warmed serving dish. Cook the pasta until al dente, then drain and add to the squash.

Meanwhile, heat the oil in a large frying pan over a medium heat. Add the sliced onion and cook gently for about 10 to 15 minutes until soft and lightly browned, then add the garlic. Stir to combine and cook for another minute or so.

Finally, add the sage, gorgonzola and cream to the frying pan and turn down the heat. Stir gently to melt the cheese and warm the cream. Add a few grinds of black pepper, taste then spoon the mixture over the pasta. Stir gently to combine. Serve with a crisp green salad.

TAGLIATELLE WITH SMOKED SALMON, CREME FRAICHE & GREEN VEGETABLES

SERVES 4-6

A tasty, easy meal that we always love and one of Isabella's particular favourites! The salmon has a smoky, salty flavour that is perfect with the creamy sauce and fresh green vegetables. I've used diced courgettes and sliced runner beans as alternatives to peas and asparagus before. This sauce also works well with egg tagliatelle which has a richer flavour and texture.

INGREDIENTS

400g tagliatelle

100g petits pois

100g fine green beans or asparagus

1 tbsp olive oil

3 cloves of garlic, finely chopped

200g smoked salmon trimmings

300ml creme fraiche or soured cream

Salt and black pepper

Lemon wedges, to serve

METHOD

Start by bringing a large pan of water to the boil with a pinch of salt. Add the tagliatelle and cook until al dente which should take about 15 to 20 minutes.

Cook the petits pois and green beans or asparagus in a steamer over the boiling pasta for about 5 minutes until cooked but not too soft. Set aside to keep warm.

Meanwhile, gently heat the oil in a large frying pan or saucepan. Add the chopped garlic and smoked salmon. Stir to warm through for a minute or two then add the creme fraiche or soured cream. Stir until the creme fraiche has melted to make a sauce. Taste then add salt and pepper if needed.

Drain the tagliatelle and transfer to a warmed serving dish with the vegetables. Spoon the sauce over the pasta and serve with lemon wedges.

BROCCOLI, RICOTTA & TOMATO PASTA SALAD

SERVES 4-6

I love this combination of flavours and colours for a light meal on a warm day. The creamy, fresh-tasting ricotta blends the more pungent flavours of garlic, chilli and olives together very well with tenderstem broccoli and crunchy pine nuts. Any short pasta shape works well with this topping.

INGREDIENTS

400g penne or rigatoni pasta

400g tenderstem broccoli

3 tbsp olive oil

400g baby plum tomatoes

3 cloves of garlic, finely sliced

½ tsp red chilli flakes

50g pine nuts

250g ricotta

25-30 green olives, pitted and halved

Freshly ground black pepper

Extra-virgin olive oil, to drizzle

METHOD

Start by bringing a large pan of salted water to the boil. Add the pasta and cook until al dente. Cut the broccoli into bite-size pieces and steam them over the boiling pasta water for 1 to 2 minutes until just cooked.

Drain the pasta then cool that and the broccoli to room temperature under cold running water. Drain well then transfer to a large serving bowl.

Next, heat the olive oil in a frying pan, add the baby tomatoes whole and heat for a minute. Then add the garlic, chilli and pine nuts. Stir and cook for another minute, making sure the garlic doesn't burn but the tomatoes become juicy.

Remove the pan from the heat, add the ricotta and olives, stir briefly, grind in some black pepper then spoon the mixture evenly over the pasta and broccoli.

Drizzle a little extra-virgin olive oil over the dish to serve.

PASTA & BEAN SALAD WITH LEMON & MINT DRESSING

SERVES 4-6

This salad is attractive, satisfying and nutritious. The light lemony dressing lifts the flavours of the beans. I tend to use frozen beans (green, broad and edamame) for speed. It's also very tasty served with sliced boiled ham or poached salmon.

INGREDIENTS

400g mixed cooked beans (borlotti, cannellini, haricot)

100g fine green beans

100g conchigliette (tiny pasta shells) or another tiny pasta

100g broad beans or edamame beans

1 large salad tomato

2 spring onions, finely chopped

For the dressing

6 tbsp extra-virgin olive oil

1 lemon, zested and juiced

1 tbsp cider vinegar

1 tsp caster sugar

¼ tsp fine salt

4 tbsp finely chopped mint leaves

METHOD

To start with, if you're using dried beans then soak them overnight and cook according to the packet instructions. If you have a mixture of tinned beans, just drain and rinse them thoroughly.

Cut the fine green beans into approximately 3cm pieces. Bring a saucepan of water to the boil and add the tiny pasta. Stir to prevent the pasta sticking on the bottom, cook until almost done then add the chopped green beans and the broad or edamame beans. Bring back to the boil for just 1 to 2 minutes until the beans and pasta are cooked but still al dente. Drain and cool them all quickly under cold running water. Finely dice the tomato then mix it with the spring onions, beans and pasta.

For the dressing

In a small bowl or jug, whisk the oil with three tablespoons of lemon juice and all the zest, vinegar, sugar and salt until combined. Stir in the chopped mint leaves then taste and adjust the seasoning if needed.

Pour the dressing over the prepared salad in a serving bowl and mix well. Refrigerate until needed.

SPICED...
FLAVOURS FROM AFAR

From saffron to turmeric and basil to coriander, spices and herbs have well known health-giving benefits. It's lucky for us that they also taste so good! They lend such characterful flavours to our favourite dishes and can transport our taste buds to far-flung destinations.

SPICED COUSCOUS WITH ROASTED VEGETABLES,
FETA & PUMPKIN SEEDS

TURKEY CHILLI WITH BLACK BEANS & LIME

VEGETABLE & CASHEW NUT STIR-FRY

MOROCCAN-STYLE CHICKEN STEW

POTATO & CHICKPEA CURRY WITH
SPINACH & COCONUT MILK

THAI-STYLE BEEF SALAD WITH NOODLES

NACHOS WITH BLACK BEANS, AVOCADO
& SWEETCORN SALSA

SALMON WITH GINGER, LIME, HONEY & SOY

RATATOUILLE

TUNA STEAKS WITH SWEET ONIONS,
SPINACH & CHICKPEAS

SPICED COUSCOUS WITH ROASTED VEGETABLES, FETA & PUMPKIN SEEDS

SERVES 4-6

So colourful and tasty with a lovely contrast of flavours, this meal is easy to cook and assemble. It can be served hot or cold.

INGREDIENTS

2 large peppers (red, yellow or both)

2 courgettes (approx. 500g)

2 red onions

300g cherry or baby plum tomatoes

2 tbsp vegetable oil

250g couscous

2 tsp smoked paprika

½ tsp ground cumin

Pinch of red chilli flakes or cayenne pepper

Salt and freshly ground black pepper

400ml vegetable or chicken stock

30g pumpkin seeds

200g feta cheese

Lemon wedges, to serve

You will need one large or two small roasting trays and a large bowl. Preheat the oven to Gas Mark 6 or 200°c.

METHOD

Start by preparing the vegetables. Chop the peppers and courgettes into bite-size pieces so they are roughly equal in size to the cherry tomatoes. This will give you evenly roasted vegetables.

Peel and chop the onions into quarters or sixths and separate their layers a little. Add them to the roasting tin with the peppers, courgettes and whole tomatoes. Drizzle over one tablespoon of the oil, stir and toss all the vegetables to coat them well, then roast in the preheated oven for 20 to 30 minutes. Stir after 10 to 15 minutes to ensure the vegetables cook evenly.

Meanwhile, weigh the couscous into a large bowl then add the smoked paprika, cumin, chilli and a few grinds of black pepper. Stir briefly to combine. Add the hot stock to the bowl and leave for 5 minutes for the couscous to soak up all the liquid and spices.

Drizzle the remaining vegetable oil over the couscous then fluff it up with a fork to separate the grains. Taste and add salt and more pepper if needed.

Put the pumpkin seeds into a small ovenproof dish or tin and toast them in the hot oven for 2 to 3 minutes. You will hear them 'popping' in the heat.

When the vegetables and pumpkin seeds are ready, remove them from the oven and carefully tip the hot vegetables over the couscous. Crumble the feta cheese on top followed by the pumpkin seeds. Serve hot or cold with the fresh lemon wedges for squeezing over the top.

TURKEY CHILLI WITH BLACK BEANS & RICE

SERVES 4

A vibrant, flavoursome meal that we all love. Add extra chilli or pickled jalapenos if you like it spicy.

INGREDIENTS

1 tbsp vegetable oil

1 red onion, chopped

1 red pepper, chopped

500g minced turkey breast and thigh

2 cloves of garlic, finely chopped

1 tin of chopped tomatoes (400g)

1 tbsp tomato puree

1 tbsp smoked paprika

1 tsp red chilli flakes

1 tsp dried oregano

½ tsp sugar

Salt and black pepper

200-250g rice

200-250g cooked black beans

Large handful of fresh coriander, chopped

2 limes, halved

METHOD

Start by heating the oil in a large pan, then slowly fry the onion and red pepper for 5 minutes until soft. Add the minced turkey and cook for a further 5 minutes.

Add the garlic, tomatoes, tomato puree, smoked paprika, chilli, oregano, sugar and a pinch of salt and pepper. Stir well, put a lid on the pan and bring to a gentle simmer. Cook for about 20 minutes, stirring occasionally.

Meanwhile, cook the rice in a pan of salted boiling water. Add the black beans to the rice towards the end of the cooking time so they just heat through. Drain the rice and beans then transfer them into a warmed serving dish.

Taste the turkey chilli and add more spice, salt and pepper if needed. Serve the chilli, rice and beans scattered with the fresh coriander and the lime juice squeezed over the top.

VEGETABLE & CASHEW NUT STIR-FRY

SERVES 4-6

I love the flavour and texture of the cashew nuts in this stir-fry, and they are a great source of vegetarian protein. The root ginger and fresh coriander are good for our digestive health and taste great too. Serve with either rice or egg noodles.

INGREDIENTS

1 tbsp vegetable or rice bran oil

1 tbsp sesame oil

1 red bell pepper, finely sliced

1 bunch of spring onions, finely sliced (approx. 80g)

2 carrots, finely sliced or in matchsticks

2 pak choi or 200g spring greens, sliced

100-120g baby corn, halved lengthways

300g beansprouts

30g (approx. 5cm) fresh root ginger, peeled and finely chopped

200g cashew nuts

2 tbsp fish sauce

3 tbsp light soy sauce

1 fresh red chilli or ¼ tsp crushed red chillies

Large handful of fresh coriander, chopped

METHOD

Heat both the oils together in a wok or large frying pan, then add all the vegetables and beansprouts. Toss to cook evenly on a medium to high heat for 5 minutes.

Add the ginger to the wok along with the cashew nuts, then stir in the fish sauce, soy sauce and chilli.

Keep stirring while it cooks for a few more minutes. Finally, add the fresh coriander and serve immediately with rice or egg noodles.

MOROCCAN-STYLE CHICKEN STEW

SERVES 6-8

This dish is inspired by the cuisine of north Africa which I just love, with colours and flavours that are both rich and vibrant, spicy and fruity. If you have time to marinate the chicken overnight, it helps the flavours develop beautifully. There is plenty of sauce with this recipe, so serve with couscous, rice or flatbreads to mop up the juices.

INGREDIENTS

For the marinade

6 cloves of garlic, peeled

1 tsp fine sea salt

5 tsp ground cumin

2 tsp mild smoked paprika

1 tsp hot paprika or red chilli flakes

¼ tsp freshly ground black pepper

1 lemon, juiced (approx. 2 tbsp)

3 tbsp rapeseed oil

For the stew

1.2-1.4kg skinless chicken thighs

1 large pinch saffron strands (approx. ¼ tsp)

2 tbsp tomato puree

250ml chicken stock

2 onions, sliced

2 red and green peppers, sliced

100g ready-to-eat dried apricots, roughly chopped

1 tin of chickpeas, drained and rinsed (240g drained weight)

Large handful fresh coriander, chopped

METHOD

For the marinade

Firstly, prepare the marinade by bashing the skinless garlic cloves in a pestle and mortar with the salt until soft and juicy. Add the cumin, smoked paprika, hot paprika or chilli, black pepper, lemon juice and oil then stir well to make a thick sauce.

In a large bowl or tub, arrange the chicken thighs in one layer then pour the marinade over them, coating each piece thoroughly on all sides. Cover and refrigerate for 1 hour, or overnight if you have time.

For the stew

When you're ready to cook, stir the saffron strands and tomato puree into the hot stock. Put the onions, peppers, apricots, chickpeas and stock into a large saucepan with a lid. This also works well in a slow cooker. Lay the marinated chicken pieces on top along with any excess marinade.

Cover with a lid and cook for about 1 hour on a low to medium heat, checking and stirring halfway through, until the chicken is well done and the vegetables are soft. You may want to leave the lid ajar towards the end of the cooking time to reduce the sauce a little. Taste and check the seasoning.

Scatter the chopped coriander on top before serving the stew with rice, couscous or flatbreads.

POTATO & CHICKPEA CURRY WITH SPINACH & COCONUT MILK

SERVES 4-6

This lightly spiced, creamy vegetable curry is very comforting and warming. I often add a little extra cumin, as I love its earthy flavour. Serve with brown basmati rice or flatbreads. If you have leftovers, the flavour of this curry is often better the day after cooking.

INGREDIENTS

1 tbsp vegetable oil

1 onion, finely chopped

600-700g all-purpose potatoes

1½ tbsp garam masala or a mixture of ground cumin, coriander, ginger, cinnamon and allspice

1 tsp chilli flakes

1 tin of coconut milk (400ml)

2 carrots, diced

1 red pepper, sliced

2 cloves of garlic, finely chopped

1 tin of chickpeas, drained and rinsed (240g drained weight)

100g baby leaf spinach

1 tsp salt

Handful of fresh coriander, roughly chopped

METHOD

Start by heating the oil in a large pan. Add the onion and fry on a low heat for about 5 to 10 minutes until soft. Meanwhile, peel and dice the potatoes into roughly 2cm cubes.

Add the garam masala, chilli, diced potatoes, coconut milk, carrots, pepper and garlic. Stir briefly then put a lid on the pan, turn up the heat and bring to a gentle simmer for 20 to 30 minutes until the potatoes and carrots are cooked.

Finally, add the drained chickpeas, spinach and salt then cook for another minute or so to wilt the leaves. Taste and adjust the seasoning, then serve the curry with rice or flatbreads and the fresh coriander scattered on top.

THAI-STYLE BEEF SALAD WITH NOODLES

SERVES 4

This tasty, crunchy and fragrant salad can be made with turkey mince or a vegetarian alternative instead of beef, if you prefer. Add fresh chillies too if you like it spicy and serve at a cool temperature, to retain the crunch of the vegetables. This recipe also works well with rice noodles.

INGREDIENTS

2 tbsp sesame oil

400-500g minced beef steak

1 red pepper, sliced into thin strips

4 spring onions, thinly sliced

2 cloves of garlic, finely chopped or minced

150-200g beansprouts

3 tbsp light soy sauce

1 tbsp fish sauce

½ tsp red chilli flakes

250g medium egg noodles

25-30g fresh coriander, roughly chopped

2-3 limes, halved

METHOD

Start by heating the sesame oil in a large frying pan. Add the minced beef, break it up into small pieces with a spoon or spatula and cook until nicely browned.

Add the red pepper, spring onions, garlic and beansprouts. Then add the soy sauce, fish sauce and chilli. Stir well to combine and cook for just 2 to 3 more minutes to keep the vegetables crunchy.

Take the pan off the heat and leave to cool a little. Meanwhile, cook the egg noodles in a pan of boiling water then drain them and cool under cold running water.

Transfer the noodles into a large serving bowl, top with the stir-fried beef and vegetables then add the fresh coriander. Serve each plateful with half a lime on the side, to squeeze over generously.

NACHOS WITH BLACK BEANS, AVOCADO & SWEETCORN SALSA

SERVES 4

The inspiration for this dish comes from Mexican Snacks by Marlena Spieler, who makes delicious authentic recipes. The black bean topping for this nacho dish can be made in advance, and in fact the flavour often benefits from keeping. It's a favourite Friday night sharing meal for us.

INGREDIENTS

For the black beans

1 tbsp vegetable oil

1 onion, chopped

400-500g cooked black beans

2 cloves of garlic, finely chopped

1 tin of chopped tomatoes (400g)

1 tbsp tomato puree

2 tsp smoked paprika

1 tsp dried thyme

¼ tsp caster sugar

Salt and black pepper

For the sweetcorn salsa

200g sweetcorn kernels

2 spring onions, finely sliced

2 salad tomatoes, finely chopped

1-2 red or green chillies, finely chopped

Large handful of fresh coriander, chopped

1 lime, juiced

Pinch of sugar

To serve

2 ripe avocados

1 bag of lightly salted corn tortilla chips

200ml soured cream

50g cheddar cheese, grated

METHOD

For the black beans

Start by heating the oil in a large frying pan, then cook the onion until soft. Add the black beans, garlic, tinned tomatoes, tomato puree, smoked paprika, thyme, sugar, salt and black pepper.

Stir to mix everything well then leave it to cook for 20 to 25 minutes until the mixture is soft and thickened. Taste and add more salt and pepper if needed. Put to one side until ready to use.

For the sweetcorn salsa

Combine the sweetcorn with all the freshly chopped ingredients in a bowl, using more or less chilli depending on how spicy you'd like the salsa. Pour over the juice from the lime, add a little salt and the sugar. Stir the salsa then cover and set aside for the flavours to infuse.

To serve

When you're almost ready to eat, preheat a grill or top oven. You'll need a large, wide serving dish to build the nachos in. Halve the avocados, remove the stones, peel off the skin or scoop out the flesh then slice thinly. Assemble the tortilla chips in an even layer over the base of the serving dish. Spoon the warm black bean mixture over the top followed by slices of avocado and an even layer of sweetcorn salsa. Put dollops of soured cream on top followed by a good scattering of grated cheese. Melt the cheese under the hot grill for a couple of minutes until golden brown. Serve immediately.

SALMON WITH GINGER, LIME, HONEY & SOY

SERVES 4

These Asian-inspired sweet, salty and sour flavours complement the richness of the salmon very well. This is one of our favourite salmon dishes. I always make plenty of the marinade as it doubles as a sauce to drizzle over vegetables and rice. Lightly steamed asparagus is also a delicious accompaniment, when it's in season.

INGREDIENTS

30g (approx. 5cm) fresh root ginger, peeled and finely grated

2 limes, zested and juiced

4 tbsp clear runny honey

5 tbsp light soy sauce

4 salmon fillets

1 tbsp sesame oil

METHOD

Preheat the oven to Gas Mark 4 or 180°c unless you have time to marinate the salmon before cooking.

Start by putting the grated ginger in a small bowl with the lime zest and juice, honey and soy sauce. Stir everything together well then taste. Add more soy sauce if you want more saltiness and more honey for extra sweetness.

If you have time and for the best flavour, put the salmon fillets into a small tray or shallow bowl and pour the marinade over them, coating each side well. Leave for at least 1 hour, covered and in the fridge, to marinate. If you are really short on time, you can skip straight to the cooking part below.

Drizzle the sesame oil over the base of an ovenproof dish and place the salmon fillets on top. Pour the marinade over the salmon and bake in the preheated oven for 15 to 20 minutes.

Serve the salmon with the hot marinade drizzled over the top, with steamed green vegetables and rice.

RATATOUILLE

SERVES 4-6

This is my version of the classic Mediterranean vegetable stew. I make it often, especially in mid to late summer when courgettes and peppers are ripe and tasty. I usually serve it with pasta or baked potatoes but it's also a very good accompaniment to a 'minute' steak or grilled chicken fillet.

INGREDIENTS

2 courgettes (approx. 450g)

1 aubergine (approx. 250g)

1 large red bell pepper

2 tbsp olive oil

1 red onion, roughly chopped

3 cloves of garlic, sliced

1 tin of chopped tomatoes (400g)

60-70g green olives, pitted and rinsed

1 tbsp tomato puree

½ tsp oregano

¼ tsp red chilli flakes

Pinch of sugar

Salt and black pepper

Large handful of fresh basil leaves, shredded

METHOD

Chop the courgettes, aubergine and red pepper into bite-size pieces or slices if you prefer. Simply heat the oil in a large frying pan or saucepan, fry the onion for 2 to 3 minutes until soft, then add all the other ingredients except the basil leaves.

Stir the sauce to combine everything, put a lid on the pan and bring to a gentle simmer. Cook for 15 to 20 minutes or until the vegetables are softened but still have some texture. Taste and adjust the seasoning, then add the shredded basil leaves just before serving.

TUNA STEAKS WITH SWEET ONIONS, SPINACH & CHICKPEAS

SERVES 4-6

A very tasty yet nutritious meal that's easy to cook in one pan. It was inspired by the Spanish flavours of mild onions, sweet ripe tomatoes, my favourite smoked paprika and fresh tuna which is a real treat for us. Serve with rice or couscous.

INGREDIENTS

3 tbsp vegetable oil

3 large mild onions, thinly sliced

4-6 cloves of garlic, thinly sliced

1 tin of chickpeas, drained and rinsed (240g drained weight)

1 tin of chopped tomatoes (400g)

1 tsp smoked paprika

½ tsp salt

½ tsp sugar

200g baby spinach leaves

4-6 fresh tuna steaks

Freshly ground black pepper

METHOD

Start by heating the oil in a large frying pan with a lid. Add the onions and cook on a medium heat, stirring now and then for about 15 to 20 minutes until they are soft and golden. Add the garlic halfway through this time to cook gently.

Add the chickpeas, tomatoes, smoked paprika, salt and sugar. Stir to combine then add the spinach leaves in a layer over the sauce. Put the tuna steaks on top, season with black pepper and cook with the lid on for 5 minutes, or until the tuna is firm and cooked through and the spinach has wilted.

Taste the sauce and add more seasoning if needed, then serve with rice or couscous.

COMFORT...
FOOD FOR COLDER DAYS

When the days get shorter and the temperature drops, I turn to food and drinks
that make me feel warm and cosy.

SWISS-STYLE CHEESE FONDUE

SLOW COOKED SMOKY PULLED PORK

RED BEAN & VEGETABLE GOULASH
WITH DUMPLINGS & SOURED CREAM

ROAST CHICKEN WITH SWEET POTATOES,
LEMON, HONEY & THYME

CHEESY POLENTA WITH SMOKY BEANS

CHEDDAR & ROOT VEGETABLE CRUMBLE

SAFFRON RISOTTO WITH PEAS & PRAWNS

SWEET ONION & POTATO PUFF PASTRY TART

BRAISED BEEF WITH TOMATOES & RED WINE

HOT ORANGE & GRAPEFRUIT PUNCH

WINTER COLESLAW

DAMSON BRANDY

WARM SPICED NUTS & SEEDS

TOMATO & GINGER RELISH

SWISS-STYLE CHEESE FONDUE

SERVES 4-6

A traditional winter sharing meal, best enjoyed when it's cold outside and warm indoors. Raclette is an excellent cheese for melting, but you can use Emmental if raclette is unavailable. The gruyère lends a rich, nutty flavour and the wine adds a balancing fruity acidity to this indulgent fondue.

INGREDIENTS

1 clove of garlic

300g raclette or Emmental

300g gruyère

300ml dry white wine

4 tbsp cornflour

Pinch of grated nutmeg

METHOD

You'll need a fondue pot or a sturdy saucepan and some long forks. You can serve this with crusty bread, cool boiled baby potatoes, cocktail gherkins, small pickled onions, cocktail sausages, chunks of cooked ham or salami and a selection of fresh salad and fruit such as carrots, peppers, mushrooms, celery, apple and pear slices. A leafy green side salad is another refreshing option.

Start by peeling and crushing the clove of garlic. Rub the crushed garlic clove around the inside of the fondue pot then set aside for another recipe. You want a hint of garlic in the fondue, not chunks.

Grate or finely chop the cheeses, discarding any hard rinds. Put the fondue pot on a medium heat. I usually start the melting process with the pot on a gas ring, followed by the traditional tabletop flame to finish off the fondue and keep it warm. Alternatively, all the melting and stirring can be done at the table over the fondue burner.

Add the cheeses and wine to the pot, then stir continuously until melted and hot. This can take about 10 minutes. If you've used Emmental cheese with the gruyère it may be in a ball at this point, which is fine! Meanwhile, prepare your chosen accompaniments and put them into bowls on the table.

Put the cornflour into a small bowl or mug with the nutmeg, add three tablespoons of water and stir to combine then quickly add the paste to the fondue pot. Stir and turn up the heat a little to help the mixture blend and thicken.

When the fondue is ready, transfer the pot to the table-top warmer and let everyone dig in with the long forks and chosen accompaniments.

SLOW COOKED SMOKY PULLED PORK

SERVES 6-8

Slow cooking is one of my favourite things for cold days. Smoked paprika and a pinch of chilli are perfect partners to rich meaty flavours. I've used this marinade on a slow cooked joint of beef before, which is also delicious. Another variation we love is to spread the marinade over skinless chicken pieces and bake them in the oven. Serve this pulled pork version in wholemeal wraps or flatbreads with bitter salad leaves, or alongside sweet potato wedges and a crunchy winter coleslaw.

INGREDIENTS

1.5-2kg pork shoulder, boneless and trimmed of skin and excess fat

100ml cider vinegar

3 tbsp tomato puree

3 tbsp soft light brown sugar

2 tbsp vegetable oil

2 tbsp mild smoked paprika

½ tsp red chilli flakes or ¼ tsp hot chilli powder

¼ tsp sea salt

Freshly ground black pepper

METHOD

You will need either a large slow cooker or an ovenproof dish with a lid. Preheat the oven to Gas Mark 3 or 160°c. Alternatively, set up the slow cooker according to the manufacturer's recommendations. I use a 5 litre capacity slow cooker pot set on high for the first hour, then switched to low for the remaining cooking time.

Simply put the pork shoulder into the cooking dish with one or two tablespoons of hot water. In a small bowl, mix together all the other ingredients to make a thick, pourable paste. Spread this paste all over the pork, then put the lid on and leave it to cook in the preheated oven or slow cooker for 4 to 5 hours, until the meat is tender and falling apart.

Shred the cooked meat with two forks and serve drizzled with the rich juices. It's great in wholemeal wraps or flatbreads with bitter salad leaves, or alongside sweet potato wedges and a crunchy winter coleslaw.

RED BEAN & VEGETABLE GOULASH WITH DUMPLINGS & SOURED CREAM

SERVES 6

Rich with smoked paprika and tomato, this vegetable casserole topped with fluffy dumplings is perfect for a cold blustery day. I often use a mixture of pre-prepared butternut squash and sweet potato, kept in the freezer, for ease.

INGREDIENTS

For the goulash

2 red onions, sliced

2 fat cloves of garlic, finely chopped

1 stick of celery, chopped

1 large carrot, peeled and diced

2 red peppers, sliced

1 large sweet potato (approx.500g)

1 tin of chopped tomatoes (400g)

500g passata

2 tins of red kidney beans, drained and rinsed (480g drained weight)

100ml warm water

1 tbsp smoked sweet paprika

1 tsp hot paprika

1 tsp fennel seeds

Sea salt and freshly ground black pepper

150-200g savoy cabbage, finely sliced

Soured cream, to serve

For the dumplings

100g vegetable suet

200g self-raising flour

100-150ml cold water

Pinch of sea salt

METHOD

For the goulash

Simply put all the vegetables (except the cabbage) into a saucepan with a lid or a slow cooker pot. If you are not using pre-prepared sweet potato, peel and chop it into bite-size cubes. Add the tinned tomatoes, passata, kidney beans, warm water, spices and seasoning to the vegetables.

Bring the goulash to a slow simmer, stir to prevent anything sticking, cover with a lid and cook for about 45 minutes until the vegetables are soft. For a slow cooker, leave on a low heat for 4 to 5 hours until the vegetables are soft and the liquid is bubbling.

For the dumplings

Meanwhile, combine the suet, flour, water and salt in a bowl to make a soft, lumpy dough. Add more water if needed but be careful it doesn't become sticky.

When the goulash is hot and the vegetables are cooked, put the finely shredded savoy cabbage in a layer over the top. Next, take a large metal spoon and divide the dumpling mixture into six evenly-sized pieces. Lay them carefully on top of the cabbage, spacing them out equally. Cover the pan or pot with the lid and cook for 20 minutes until the dumplings are steamed and well risen.

Serve the goulash and dumplings with a generous spoonful of soured cream for each bowl.

ROAST CHICKEN WITH SWEET POTATOES, LEMON, HONEY & THYME

SERVES 4

This is an easy dish as everything cooks together, with the juices melting into the vegetables to create a delicious fragrant sauce in the bottom of the roasting tin. At the same time, the chicken skin becomes crisp and the meat tender, all infused with lemon, honey and thyme.

INGREDIENTS

500g sweet potatoes (approx. 2 large or 4 small)

2 onions

1 large or 2 small unwaxed lemons

800g chicken thighs and drumsticks, skin on (approx. 4-6 pieces)

3 tbsp cold-pressed rapeseed oil

3 tbsp runny honey

1 tsp dried thyme

½ tsp sea salt

Freshly ground black pepper

METHOD

Preheat the oven to Gas Mark 4 or 180°c. Firstly, peel and wash the sweet potatoes then cut them into 2 or 3cm chunks. Put them into a roasting tin in one layer.

Next, peel the onions and chop them into quarters, roughly separating the layers into evenly-sized pieces. Add them to the roasting tin.

Wash the lemons then thinly slice them into rounds less than 1cm thick, discarding any pips. Arrange the lemon slices evenly over the sweet potatoes and onions in the roasting tin.

Lay the chicken pieces on top of the lemon slices, skin side upwards. In a small bowl, combine the rapeseed oil, honey, thyme, salt and pepper. Spoon this mixture over the chicken and vegetables to give everything an even coating.

Place the roasting tin in the centre of the preheated oven for 35 to 45 minutes and cook uncovered until the chicken skins are crisp and golden and the vegetables are soft. Check halfway through the roasting time to make sure the sweet potatoes and onions are cooking evenly.

Serve with steamed green vegetables such as spinach, chard or purple sprouting broccoli.

CHEESY POLENTA WITH SMOKY BEANS

SERVES 4

This is a favourite meal of ours for a comforting, warming teatime. The smoky beans can be made in advance then reheated but are very quick anyway. The polenta needs to be made last and served straight from the pan for a soft texture.

INGREDIENTS

1 tbsp vegetable oil

1 onion

400g mixed cooked beans (cannellini, kidney, borlotti, flageolet, butter)

1 tin of chopped tomatoes (400g)

1 tbsp tomato puree

1 tbsp dark brown sugar

1 tbsp sweet smoked paprika

1 tbsp chopped rosemary

Salt and black pepper

800ml vegetable stock

200g polenta

100g mature cheddar cheese

25g salted butter

METHOD

Heat the oil in a large frying pan or saucepan with a lid. Start by finely chopping the onion and frying gently in the oil until soft.

Add the mixed beans, tinned tomatoes, tomato puree, dark brown sugar, smoked paprika and rosemary to the onions. Stir well then put a lid on the pan and turn up the heat to a gentle simmer. Cook for 10 to 15 minutes then stir again, taste and add salt and black pepper if needed. Take the pan off the heat and set aside until the polenta is ready.

Put the vegetable stock into a large saucepan and bring to the boil. Stir the stock while you pour the polenta into it in a steady stream. Continue to stir thoroughly and quickly until the polenta thickens, then turn the heat down. Be careful as the thick, boiling polenta can bubble up and burn.

Grate the cheese into the polenta, add the butter and stir well, adding salt and pepper if needed. Serve the smoky beans on top of the soft, cheesy polenta.

CHEDDAR & ROOT VEGETABLE CRUMBLE

SERVES 4 AS A MAIN MEAL OR 6 AS AN ACCOMPANIMENT

This hearty, savoury root vegetable crumble is a family favourite. Serve it with green vegetables as a vegetarian main meal or alongside fat butcher's sausages for meat lovers. Use pre-prepared sweet potato or butternut squash for ease if you're short on time.

INGREDIENTS

300g potatoes

150-200g sweet potato or butternut squash

2 carrots

200g swede

100g garden peas

25g unsalted butter

1 leek

200g full-fat cream cheese

2 cloves of garlic, finely chopped

Pinch of salt

Freshly ground black pepper

For the crumble topping

160g plain flour

75g unsalted butter

150g mature cheddar cheese

1 tbsp finely chopped rosemary

METHOD

You'll need an ovenproof dish about 23 by 23cm and 6cm deep. Preheat the oven to Gas Mark 4 or 180°c.

Start by peeling the root vegetables (potatoes, sweet potato or squash, carrots and swede) then chopping them into bite-size chunks, approximately 2 to 3cm square.

Cook the diced vegetables in a large pan of boiling water for 10 to 15 minutes until tender. Add the peas towards the end of this cooking time to heat through. Drain the vegetables in a colander, reserving a small cupful of the cooking liquid.

Next, melt the butter in a frying pan then slice the leek and cook in the butter until soft. Take off the heat and stir in the cream cheese to make a sauce, adding a little of the reserved vegetable cooking water if it's too thick. Add the finely chopped garlic then season well with salt and black pepper.

Mix the cooked vegetables with the leek and cheese sauce and stir to coat everything well. Tip the mixture into the ovenproof dish and level out the surface. You can prepare the dish in advance to this point. Cool, cover and refrigerate until needed, then add the crumble topping and bake when you're ready.

For the crumble topping

Rub the butter into the plain flour with your fingertips until it resembles breadcrumbs. Grate the cheese and stir it in with the rosemary and a little seasoning.

Cover the creamy vegetable filling with the crumble topping in an even layer then bake in the preheated oven for 30 minutes until golden on top.

Leave the crumble to stand for a couple of minutes before serving with steamed green vegetables, sausages or both!

SAFFRON RISOTTO WITH PEAS & PRAWNS

SERVES 4-6

A satisfying one-pan meal. It does take a bit of effort to keep stirring but if you have a helper in the kitchen, all the better! The beautiful colours of golden saffron, pink prawns and bright green little peas make me smile.

INGREDIENTS

1 onion

1 stick of celery

25g unsalted butter

1 tbsp olive oil

2 cloves of garlic, finely chopped

350g risotto rice (such as arborio)

200ml medium-dry white wine

1 litre hot vegetable or fish stock

2 large pinches of saffron strands

100g peas

250g large cooked prawns

METHOD

Start by finely dicing the onion and celery. Heat the butter and oil in a large pan, then add the vegetables. Cook on a low heat for 10 minutes, stirring occasionally until completely soft and lightly golden.

Add the chopped garlic then the risotto rice. Stir to coat the rice with oil and cook for another 2 minutes, then add the wine.

Turn the heat up to medium and let the wine be absorbed by the rice. Keep stirring gently. Heat the stock ready for use and add the saffron strands to infuse.

Using a ladle or small jug, add the stock to the risotto pan a bit at a time, stirring in between each addition to prevent anything sticking. Wait until the liquid has been absorbed by the rice before adding the next ladleful.

Repeat this process, stirring all the time, until the stock is used up and the rice has swollen. It should have a creamy texture; taste and add a little more hot water if the grains are still too hard in the middle. The rice should have some 'bite' or texture and must not be mushy.

Add the peas and prawns and stir to heat through. Taste the risotto for seasoning then add salt and black pepper if needed. Serve straight from the pan!

SWEET ONION & POTATO PUFF PASTRY TART

SERVES 4-6

This flat, flaky tart is a different kind to the deep-filled shortcrust variety. Comforting and moreish, the sweet onions and potatoes are complemented by the astringent rosemary and the rich creme fraiche. Use brown onions with a pinch of sugar if you can't find the large, mild Spanish ones. This tart is also very tasty with a few rashers of crispy bacon on top.

INGREDIENTS

350-400g puff pastry

500g potatoes, skins on

2 large mild onions (350-400g)

25g butter

1 tbsp vegetable or olive oil

1 tbsp chopped rosemary

Freshly ground black pepper

Pinch of salt

200ml creme fraiche

Olive oil or cold-pressed rapeseed oil

You will need one large or two small flat baking trays. Preheat the oven to Gas Mark 6 or 200°c.

METHOD

If it's not ready-rolled, start by rolling out the puff pastry on a floured surface quite thinly, making an oblong shape to fit neatly into your baking tray or trays.

Cook the potatoes, whole if small or halved if large, in a pan of boiling salted water until tender. Drain and set aside to cool a little.

Thinly slice the onions then heat the butter and oil in a pan and gently fry them until soft and golden, which should take about 15 to 20 minutes. Add the chopped rosemary to the onions with a grind of black pepper and the pinch of salt. Take the pan off the heat.

Once the potatoes are cool enough to handle, slice them (leaving the skins on) into 2cm thick discs. Place these discs onto the pastry in an even layer, going right to the edges.

Spread the onion mixture evenly over the top of the potato. With a large spoon, put dollops of the creme fraiche onto the tart followed by a grind of black pepper.

Bake the tart for 20 to 30 minutes in the preheated oven, then remove once the pastry is cooked through and leave to cool a little. Drizzle the tart with olive or rapeseed oil then serve in large squares with a simple green salad and vinaigrette.

BRAISED BEEF WITH TOMATOES & RED WINE

SERVES 6-8

A delicious, warming, slow cooked dish of Italian origins. Braising the beef makes it very tender and succulent in the rich, savoury sauce. Serve with mashed potatoes or soft polenta and green vegetables.

INGREDIENTS

1.5-2kg stewing beef joint (such as brisket)

3 tbsp olive oil

2 large onions

1 stick of celery

2 large carrots

200ml full-bodied red wine

500g passata

1 tbsp tomato puree

1 tsp sugar

2 bay leaves

1 tbsp chopped rosemary

½ tsp ground cloves or ground allspice

Salt and freshly ground black pepper

METHOD

You will need either a large ovenproof dish with a lid or a slow cooker. Preheat the oven to Gas Mark 1 or 140°c. Alternatively, set up the slow cooker according to the manufacturer's recommendations. I use a 5 litre capacity slow cooker pot set on low. Trim your beef joint of any excess fat.

Start by heating the oil in a large frying pan and browning the beef joint on all sides. This is not to cook the meat, just to seal the outside, and takes 4 to 5 minutes. Transfer the joint carefully to the casserole dish or slow cooker pot.

Next, finely dice the onions, celery and carrots. Cook them in the frying pan, stirring to coat them in the oil and meat juices for about 10 minutes or until softened. Add the red wine and bring to the boil for 5 minutes until the liquid has reduced, then add all this to the beef in the pot.

Pour the passata over the beef along with the tomato puree, sugar, herbs and cloves or allspice. Make sure the meat is well covered with sauce. Season well with salt and black pepper then put the lid back on and slowly cook in the preheated oven or using a slow cooker for 4 to 5 hours.

Taste the sauce and adjust the seasoning if needed. The meat should be meltingly tender at this point. Serve with mashed potatoes or soft polenta and green cabbage, green beans or broccoli.

HOT ORANGE & GRAPEFRUIT PUNCH

MAKES ABOUT 6 MUGS (1 LITRE)

A warming, citrussy, non-alcoholic drink that I remember from my childhood. I love the not-too-sweet zesty flavour and the subtle spices. This can be made in advance and warmed through as needed.

INGREDIENTS

3 oranges, unwaxed

1 yellow grapefruit

100g sugar

1 cinnamon stick

4 cloves

1 litre water

METHOD

Start by washing the oranges and grapefruit in hot water. Remove all the zest (just the coloured skin, not the white pith) from the oranges and the grapefruit with a sharp knife or parer. The zest doesn't need to be in neat pieces here.

Put the zest, sugar, cinnamon, cloves and water into a large saucepan. Turn on the heat to warm up the liquid gently and stir to dissolve the sugar.

Put a lid on the saucepan and leave on a low heat to infuse the zest and spices for 20 to 30 minutes. The longer you leave this mixture to warm through, the stronger and more zesty the flavours will become.

Meanwhile, squeeze the fresh juice from the zested oranges and grapefruit. Add this to the saucepan and stir again. Taste and add more sugar if needed.

Use a ladle to decant the warm punch into large mugs or punch bowls, leaving the spices and zest in the bottom of the pan. Any leftover liquid can be strained and stored in the fridge for a few days.

WINTER COLESLAW

SERVES 4-6

We love this crunchy and colourful winter salad. The dressing is based on the classic French remoulade, typically served with celeriac. I enjoy the additional flavours of tarragon and cider vinegar which add fresh and tangy elements to complement the red onion and apple. It's a great accompaniment for roast meats and seasonal root vegetables.

INGREDIENTS

200g red cabbage

200g celeriac

1 medium carrot

1 small red onion

1 small apple

For the dressing

5 tbsp mayonnaise

1½ tbsp cider vinegar

1 tbsp dried tarragon

3 tsp Dijon mustard

Freshly ground black pepper

METHOD

Simply wash and prepare then grate or finely slice the vegetables and apple into a large bowl.

In a small jug or bowl, mix all the dressing ingredients together. Taste and adjust the seasoning before adding the dressing to the vegetables.

Toss well to coat everything, then refrigerate the coleslaw until needed.

DAMSON BRANDY

My favourite warming tipple! I make this in autumn so it's ready for Christmas and New Year. In the past I've also made it with Calvados, an apple brandy which adds extra fruitiness.

INGREDIENTS

500g damsons

250g caster sugar

1 litre brandy

METHOD

You'll need a two litre wide-necked bottle with a lid or a two litre Kilner jar to keep the brandy in. Start by washing and drying the bottle or jar thoroughly.

Wash and dry the damsons, remove any stalks or leaves and check for blemishes. With a sharp knife, make a slit down the side of each damson then put them into the bottle or jar.

Tip the sugar over the damsons in the bottle then top with the brandy. Seal the lid then shake or tip the bottle gently a few times to mix the contents together. At this stage the sugar won't dissolve fully.

Over the next 2 to 3 weeks, occasionally repeat the gentle shaking or tipping to dissolve the sugar in the damson juices and alcohol.

After 1 month, the damson brandy is ready to drink but I prefer to leave it for at least 2 months as the flavour improves on keeping. Strain or decant into a smaller bottle for serving.

WARM SPICED NUTS & SEEDS

SERVES 6 AS A SNACK

Fragrant and warming with a hint of chilli, these nuts and seeds are delicious to nibble on with drinks by the fire, served warm straight from the pan.

INGREDIENTS

150g mixed whole nuts (almonds, cashews, brazils, hazelnuts, walnuts)

50g pumpkin or sunflower seeds

1 tbsp cold-pressed rapeseed oil

1 tbsp caster sugar

1 tbsp finely chopped rosemary

2 tsp coriander seeds

½ tsp fine sea salt

¼ tsp chilli flakes

Freshly ground black pepper

METHOD

Add all the ingredients to a large frying pan, then warm gently and stir for about 5 to 7 minutes until the seasonings have coated the nuts, the spices have released their aromas and everything is warmed through.

Tip the spiced nuts and seeds into a serving bowl to cool a little before eating. You might need little serviettes to wipe your fingers on!

TOMATO & GINGER RELISH

MAKES 5 JARS (340G EACH)

This relish is so very tasty, a homemade alternative to spicy ketchup! The flavour mellows over time as with all pickles and preserves. Serve with hot or cold savoury dishes.

INGREDIENTS

3 tins of chopped tomatoes (1200g)

400ml vinegar (white wine, red wine, or a mixture)

300g granulated sugar

100g fresh root ginger, peeled and roughly chopped

100g dates, pitted and chopped

4 cloves of garlic, roughly chopped

2 tsp fine salt

½ tsp cayenne pepper or red chilli flakes

½ tsp ground allspice or ¼ tsp ground cloves and ¼ tsp ground cinnamon

METHOD

You will need five medium-size jam jars or equivalent wide-necked bottles with lids and a large saucepan or preserving pan.

Wash your jam jars and lids thoroughly in hot soapy water, then leave them to dry out and keep warm on a clean baking tray in the oven, set to a very low heat.

To make the relish, simply put all of the ingredients into the pan, slowly bring to the boil and stir to dissolve the sugar and salt. Continue to simmer the mixture for 45 minutes until it is thick and has reduced by about half, stirring occasionally.

Remove the pan from the heat then carefully blend the mixture until smooth with a stick blender.

Ladle the relish into the warm jam jars or bottles. Put the lids on and leave to cool before labelling.

Store the relish in a cool place and once opened, keep in the fridge.

PUDDING...
THE PERFECT ENDING

A pudding or dessert is, for me, the perfect ending to a meal. I love fruit in sweet desserts, either cooked or fresh, to balance rich or creamy flavours and textures. I make puddings like this for special gatherings of family and friends, or if we deserve a real treat.

**BROWN SUGAR MERINGUES WITH
ORANGE-SCENTED BERRIES & CREAM**

RASPBERRY CLAFOUTIS

LEMON & PINE NUT TART

GLAZED CHOCOLATE & ALMOND CAKE

APPLE & LEMON CRUMBLE

TIRAMISU

FRUIT FOOLS

DARK CHOCOLATE & CHERRY CRISPY CAKES

SUMMER FRUIT PAVLOVA

BROWN SUGAR MERINGUES WITH ORANGE-SCENTED BERRIES & CREAM

MAKES 12 MERINGUES (SERVES 6)

These gooey meringues have a golden colour and soft centre, perfect with fragrant berries and softly whipped cream. The zesty orange and tart berries balance the sweetness of the meringue and cream perfectly. Totally delicious!

INGREDIENTS

For the meringues

2 fresh egg whites, at room temperature

60g soft light brown sugar

60g caster sugar

For the berries & cream

300g mixed berries (strawberries, blueberries, blackberries, raspberries)

1 large orange

1 tbsp caster sugar

300ml whipping cream

1 tsp icing sugar

METHOD

For the meringues

You'll need two flat baking trays lined with greaseproof paper or baking parchment. Preheat the oven to Gas Mark ¼ or 110°c.

Start by whisking the egg whites until stiff in a clean, dry bowl. Mix the two sugars together in another bowl then add them to the egg whites. Whisk again until the mixture turns shiny and forms stiff peaks. This takes about 10 minutes.

Use two dessert spoons to place small oval dollops of the mixture onto the lined baking trays, spaced a little apart. You should have twelve in total.

Bake in the preheated oven for 1½ to 2 hours until the meringues are dry and crispy on the outside. Remove from the oven and allow to cool completely before peeling them off the baking paper. Store in an airtight container in a single layer on more baking paper until needed.

For the berries & cream

If the berries are fresh, remove any stalks and cut the larger ones into evenly-sized pieces. If you are using frozen berries, defrost them in advance. Put the prepared berries into a bowl.

Zest the orange with a fine grater and set aside, then halve and juice the orange, squeezing it directly over the berries. Sprinkle the caster sugar over the berries and stir gently to combine. Set aside until needed.

In another medium-size bowl, whisk the cream until softly firm. Add the icing sugar and reserved orange zest then whisk again briefly to combine. Taste and add more icing sugar if needed.

To serve

Sandwich the meringues together in pairs with a good helping of cream between them, then top with the berries and juice.

RASPBERRY CLAFOUTIS

SERVES 4-6

A classic French baked batter pudding. Traditionally, clafoutis is made with ripe cherries but I love the tart, summery flavour of the raspberries in my version. You could use loganberries if you have them or blackberries in the early autumn.

INGREDIENTS

250g fresh raspberries

50g plain flour

Pinch of salt

80g caster sugar

3 large eggs

150ml semi-skimmed milk

1 tsp vanilla extract

1 tbsp flaked almonds

Icing sugar and single cream, to serve

You will need a well-buttered 25cm round baking dish. Preheat the oven to Gas Mark 4 or 180°c.

METHOD

Firstly, spread the raspberries out evenly in the base of your buttered dish. In a medium-size bowl, sift together the flour and salt, then stir in the sugar.

Crack the eggs into a mug or small bowl and beat together lightly with a fork. Measure the milk into a jug and add the vanilla extract.

Make a well in the centre of the flour and sugar with a wooden spoon. Add the beaten eggs and stir from the middle, drawing in the flour from the edges to make a thick batter.

Pour the milk slowly into the bowl, stirring continuously to make the batter thinner and smoother. Pour this batter carefully over the raspberries in the baking dish.

Sprinkle the flaked almonds over the top then bake the clafoutis in the preheated oven for 25 to 30 minutes. The batter should have risen around the sides and gently set in the middle, with a golden brown colour and juicy raspberries on top.

Leave the pudding to cool a little before serving with a dusting of icing sugar and a drizzle of cream.

LEMON & PINE NUT TART

SERVES 8

This recipe is adapted from one of my favourite little books, Coffee & Bites by Susie Theodorou. The sweet yet zesty lemon curd is sandwiched between crumbly pastry layers and topped with golden toasted pine nuts. I've made it time and time again; it's always delicious.

INGREDIENTS

300g plain flour, plus extra for dusting

1 tsp baking powder

100g unsalted butter

125g caster sugar

1 lemon, zested

2 eggs, beaten

310-320g lemon curd (about 1 jar of good quality shop-bought or homemade)

½ tbsp milk

50g pine nuts

Icing sugar

You will need a 23cm fluted, loose-bottomed flan ring with sides about 4 to 5cm deep. Preheat the oven to Gas Mark 4 or 180°c.

METHOD

Start by sifting the flour and baking powder into a bowl. Add the butter, cut into chunks, and rub it into the flour until it looks like fine breadcrumbs. Stir in the caster sugar, lemon zest and beaten eggs to bring the mixture into a ball of dough.

Gently knead the pastry on a floury surface until smooth then cover with cling film or greaseproof paper and chill for about 20 to 30 minutes until it's a little firmer to handle.

Lightly grease the flan ring with butter or oil and place on top of a baking tray for stability in the oven. Take two thirds of the pastry out of the fridge, dust it with flour so it's not sticky to touch, then press it into the base and 3cm up the sides of the flan ring.

Press the dough evenly into the fluted sides, then spoon the lemon curd in an even layer over the base. Dust the remaining third of the dough with flour and roll out gently into a circle, big enough to completely cover the lemon curd layer. Lay the circle over the filling then pinch the edges together as best you can to seal the pastry.

Finally, brush the milk over the top of the tart. Sprinkle the pine nuts in an even layer on top then bake in the preheated oven for 30 to 40 minutes until slightly risen, firm and golden brown.

Dust the top with icing sugar before leaving the tart to cool. Serve in wedges with whipped cream or creme fraiche.

GLAZED CHOCOLATE & ALMOND CAKE

SERVES 6-8

This is such an easy cake to make with a gorgeous, nutty texture and rich chocolate flavour. It has the added benefit of being gluten-free. I add the chocolate glaze for special occasions. I found that this cake can also be chilled in the fridge after baking which gives it a firm texture, similar to a torte, and is lovely served with fresh raspberries and cream. The recipe is adapted from 100 Desserts to Die For by Trish Deseine.

INGREDIENTS

150g dark chocolate (preferably 70% cocoa solids or more)

60ml good quality vegetable oil (cold-pressed rapeseed or sunflower oil)

3 eggs

75g caster sugar

125g ground almonds

For the chocolate glaze

150g dark chocolate (70% cocoa solids)

100g unsalted butter

Preheat the oven to Gas Mark 4 or 180°c. Line the base of a round loose-bottomed cake tin (I use a 19cm diameter tin) and then grease the insides with oil.

METHOD

Melt the chocolate gently, in a bowl in the microwave or over a pan of simmering water. Add the oil to the melted chocolate and stir to combine.

In a separate bowl, whisk the eggs with the sugar until the mixture is pale, bubbly and doubled in size. Then whisk the ground almonds into the mixture.

Add the chocolate and oil mixture to the egg, sugar and almond mixture. Gently stir together then pour into the prepared tin.

Bake for 25 to 30 minutes until the cake is set but soft in the middle. Cool completely on a wire rack before removing from the tin.

For the chocolate glaze

Break the chocolate into pieces in a microwaveable bowl, chop up the butter and add it to the bowl, then melt slowly on a low heat setting. Alternatively, place the bowl over a pan of hot (but not boiling) water and melt slowly, stirring gently until glossy and smooth.

Pour the glaze evenly over the cooled cake, letting it flow over the edges. Allow to cool again before decorating.

APPLE & LEMON CRUMBLE

SERVES 6

This delicious hot pudding is inspired by my mother-in-law Di, who is a wonderful home cook and always feeds us royally. I've used two varieties of apple to give the filling more texture as well as the zest and juice of two lemons which add a wonderful zing and lightness to the dish. I sometimes make the apple and lemon filling without the crumble as a warm fruity dessert to serve with creme fraiche. It's delicious either way.

INGREDIENTS

For the fruit filling

4 large cooking apples (approx. 1kg) such as Bramleys

4 eating or dessert apples

2 unwaxed lemons, zested and juiced

1 tbsp caster sugar (you may need more, depending on the sweetness of the apples)

For the crumble topping

200g plain flour

100g unsalted butter, chilled

70g soft light brown sugar

You will need a 22cm square or round ovenproof baking dish, with sides at least 6cm deep. Preheat the oven to Gas Mark 4 or 180°c.

METHOD

For the fruit filling

Peel and core all the apples, then cut the Bramleys into rough chunks and the eating apples into bite-size pieces. Next, cook the apples with 100ml of water in a large saucepan with the lid on for about 10 minutes until softened. Take off the heat then add the lemon zest, lemon juice and sugar. Stir well, then taste the filling and add more sugar if needed. Transfer to the ovenproof baking dish.

For the crumble topping

Weigh the flour into a large bowl, add the cold butter in small chunks and rub it in with your fingertips until the mixture resembles fine breadcrumbs. Stir in the sugar.

Sprinkle the crumble topping evenly over the fruit filling and spread it right to the edges of the dish. Bake in the middle of the preheated oven for 30 to 40 minutes until golden and bubbling.

Serve the crumble with hot custard or double cream...yum!

TIRAMISU

SERVES 6

This is the classic Italian dessert, layered like a trifle but literally translated as 'pick me up'. I use strong decaffeinated coffee from the cafetière and just a small amount of alcohol. Adding whipped egg whites to the creamy topping gives it an amazing light texture, but be aware that they are not cooked, for anyone who shouldn't eat raw eggs.

INGREDIENTS

300ml strong coffee

2 tbsp brandy or dark rum

4 tbsp caster sugar

3 eggs

1 large orange, juiced (approx. 80-100ml juice)

250g mascarpone

200g savoiardi biscuits (also known as sponge fingers or boudoir biscuits)

2 tbsp cocoa powder

You'll also need a serving bowl about 22cm in diameter and 6 to 8cm deep.

METHOD

Firstly, measure the coffee into a jug, add the brandy or rum and one tablespoon of the caster sugar. Stir the mixture to dissolve the sugar then set aside.

Separate the eggs into two bowls, one for whites and one for yolks. Whisk the egg whites until they are stiff then set aside.

Add the orange juice and the remaining sugar to the egg yolks and whisk lightly until well combined and fluffy or bubbly. Beat the mascarpone to soften it then gradually add it to the egg yolk and orange mixture, stirring well until smooth. A small whisk helps here.

Finally, gently fold the egg whites into the creamy yolk mixture with a large metal spoon.

To assemble the tiramisu, place half of the savoiardi biscuits into the serving bowl so they cover the base evenly. Slowly pour half of the coffee mixture over the biscuits, which will soak it up immediately. Next, spoon half of the creamy egg topping over the soaked biscuits. Cover evenly with a tablespoon of the finely sieved cocoa powder.

Now take the remaining savoiardi biscuits one at a time, dip them into the remaining coffee mixture fairly quickly so they soak up some liquid but don't become too soggy, and make another layer in the serving dish. Spoon the remaining creamy topping over them in an even layer, followed by a final dusting of cocoa powder.

Cover the dish and refrigerate for about 6 hours to set the tiramisu before serving.

FRUIT FOOLS

SERVES 6-8

A fruit fool is a divine and versatile combination of softly whipped cream with seasonal fruit puree. It is so easy to make with tart fresh fruit such as raspberries and blackberries, or cooked and pureed fruit such as plums, damsons, rhubarb, gooseberries or blackcurrants. Sweeten a little with sugar or flavoured syrup. Drizzle with fruit sauce and serve with crisp biscuits or layered in individual glasses with crushed meringue.

INGREDIENTS

Plum Fool

600g-700g plums

1-2 tbsp caster sugar, if needed

300ml whipping or double cream

Raspberry Fool

400g fresh raspberries

300ml whipping or double cream

Caster sugar, to taste

Fresh mint, to serve

METHOD

Plum Fool

Start by washing the plums and removing any stalks. Put them straight into a saucepan and heat very gently on a low heat, stirring occasionally until they start to release their juices. Turn up the heat and simmer gently to evaporate and concentrate the juices. This may take a few minutes.

Once the plums are completely soft and the juices have reduced, remove the pan from the heat. Leave to cool a little but while still warm, spoon the plums into a sieve over a bowl and stir well to remove the skins and stones. You should have approximately 500g of plum puree.

Taste the puree and add sugar to sweeten if needed. Set aside to cool completely. Whip the cream into soft peaks then add the plum puree and fold in gently, leaving a swirl or two. Serve the plum fool with crisp biscuits on the side.

Raspberry Fool

Put the raspberries into a bowl and crush with a fork until soft and juicy. Taste and add a spoonful of sugar if they're too tart. Stir to dissolve the sugar.

In a larger bowl, whip the cream until soft peaks form. Add the crushed raspberries to the cream and fold them in gently to create a swirl. It doesn't need to be completely mixed and you may find the cream stiffens a little more with the addition of the raspberries.

Serve the raspberry fool topped with a few sprigs of mint, either from a large bowl, or divided between individual bowls or glasses.

DARK CHOCOLATE & CHERRY CRISPY CAKES

MAKES 12

This is a richer, darker version of the simple children's party treat. Quick and easy with no baking required.

INGREDIENTS

250g dark chocolate (70% cocoa solids)

50g unsalted butter

2 tbsp golden syrup

100g puffed rice cereal

100g glacé cherries or Morello cherries if you can find them

Icing sugar and fresh cherries, to serve

METHOD

You will need a 12-hole cupcake tray and 12 paper cases. Firstly, arrange the cases in the cupcake tray. Break up the chocolate into small pieces and halve the cherries.

Put the broken up chocolate, butter and syrup into a large saucepan. Heat gently and stir continuously until fully melted.

Remove the pan from the heat then add the puffed rice and halved cherries. Stir gently but thoroughly until everything is well coated.

With a small spoon, fill the cupcake cases to the brim then leave to cool and set. Serve dusted with icing sugar and a fresh cherry on the side.

SUMMER FRUIT PAVLOVA

SERVES 8-10

This is such a gorgeous special occasion dessert. Crisp sweet meringue, juicy ripe fruit, softly whipped cream and tangy fruit curd. I make it rectangular in shape so it's a little easier to serve in slices. The raspberry sauce can be made in advance and is also delicious served with other puddings or cakes.

INGREDIENTS

For the meringue

4 fresh egg whites, at room temperature

160g caster sugar

For the raspberry sauce

400g raspberries, fresh or frozen

1-2 tbsp icing sugar

To assemble and serve

300ml whipping cream

1 x 310g jar of fruit curd (passionfruit or lemon) or 4 tbsp apricot conserve

3-4 ripe peaches or nectarines

1 punnet of strawberries

1 punnet of raspberries

Mint leaves or edible flowers (nasturtiums, marigolds, rose petals) for garnish

METHOD

For the meringue

Preheat the oven to Gas Mark 2 or 150°c. Line three baking sheets with baking parchment or greaseproof paper. Draw a 12 by 24cm rectangle in pencil on one side of the paper then turn it over.

Put the egg whites and caster sugar in a spotlessly clean metal or glass bowl and whisk on full speed until the mixture is fluffy and forming stiff, dry peaks. This takes about 10 minutes. Divide the mixture between the prepared baking sheets, carefully smoothing it over the rectangular templates with the back of a metal spoon or palette knife. Bake immediately for 45 to 60 minutes or until crisp. Turn off the oven and leave the meringue inside until cool. Then transfer onto a wire rack and carefully remove the baking paper.

For the raspberry sauce

If you are using frozen raspberries, defrost them in advance. In a large bowl or jug, puree the raspberries until smooth. Stir the pureed raspberries through a sieve over a bowl, then add a tablespoon of icing sugar and stir well. Taste and add more sugar if needed, then refrigerate.

To assemble and serve

Whip the cream until soft peaks form, then swirl the fruit curd or apricot conserve through the cream, creating a marbled effect. Thinly slice the peaches or nectarines. Halve the strawberries if they are large and check the fresh raspberries are all clean and dry.

Now you're ready to assemble the pavlova. Dollop some of the marbled fruit cream onto your serving plate then put the first meringue rectangle on top to hold it in place. Spread a third of the fruit cream on top followed by some peach or nectarine slices, raspberries, strawberries and a drizzle of raspberry sauce. Top with the second meringue layer and repeat, but save plenty of the fruit for the top layer. When the pavlova is assembled, drizzle a little raspberry sauce over the top and add some mint leaves or edible flowers for garnish. Serve with the remaining raspberry sauce on the side in a little jug.

CONVERSION TABLES

Oven Temperature

Setting the oven to the correct temperature for baked foods is important for the best results.

The oven I have used to create these recipes is a standard gas oven. If you use a fan-assisted oven you may need to reduce the cooking time and/or the oven temperature for baked recipes.

GAS MARK	CELCIUS	FAHRENHEIT
1	140	275
2	150	300
3	160	325
4	180	350
5	190	375
6	200	400
7	210	425
8	220	450
9	240	475

Measurements

LIQUIDS	METRIC EQUIVALENT
1 teaspoon (tsp)	5ml
1 tablespoon (tbsp)	15ml
1 pint	600ml
WEIGHTS	**METRIC EQUIVALENT**
1 ounce (oz)	30g
1 pound (lb)	450g

A NOTE ON INGREDIENTS

Eggs

I use large, fresh, free-range chicken eggs.

Butter

I use unsalted butter unless I've suggested otherwise in a recipe.

Milk

I use semi-skimmed cow's milk unless I've suggested otherwise. Alternative or non-dairy milks can usually be substituted in my recipes.

Citrus Fruits

I always use unwaxed lemons, limes and oranges.

Serving Sizes

My portion sizes tend to be generous as all my recipes have been tasted by families with good appetites. If you have leftovers, the vast majority of the dishes in this book will keep well in the fridge or an airtight container for baked goods, to serve the next day. Alternatively, freeze in portions to keep for longer.

INDEX

Cheddar & Root Vegetable Crumble 152
Braised Beef with Tomatoes & Red Wine 158
Winter Coleslaw 160

Cashew nuts
Vegetable & Cashew Nut Stir-Fry 125
Warm Spiced Nuts & Seeds 162

Cauliflower
Creamy Cauliflower & Garlic Soup 74

Celeriac
Winter Coleslaw 160

Celery
Spiced Red Lentil Soup 67
Roast Pumpkin & Pasta Soup with Garlic,
Chilli & Thyme 72
Vegetable Stock 76
Chicken Stock 76
Linguine with Aubergine & Sun-Dried
Tomato Sauce 104
Conchiglie with Vegetable & Lentil Ragu 106
Homemade Tomato Sauce for Pasta 107
Beef Ragu with Gnocchi 108
Swiss-Style Cheese Fondue 142
Red Bean & Vegetable Goulash with
Dumplings & Soured Cream 146
Saffron Risotto with Peas & Prawns 154
Braised Beef with Tomatoes & Red Wine 158

Cheddar
Spinach & Cheese Scramble 22
Breakfast Potato Omelette 24
Cheese Scones 54
Savoury Turkey Rolls & Rainbow Coleslaw 80
Nachos with Black Beans, Avocado
& Sweetcorn Salsa 132
Cheesy Polenta with Smoky Beans 150
Cheddar & Root Vegetable Crumble 152

Cherries
Warming Porridge with Almonds
& Berry Compote 16
Raspberry Clafoutis 170
Dark Chocolate & Cherry Crispy Cakes 182

Chicken
Chicken Stock 76
Poached Chicken with Green Lentils,
Watercress & Mustard Dressing 88
White Bean Salad with Rosemary
& Garlic Dressing 92
Moroccan-Style Chicken Stew 126
Ratatouille 136
Slow Cooked Smoky Pulled Pork 144
Roast Chicken with Sweet Potatoes,
Lemon, Honey & Thyme 148

Chicken Stock
Red Pepper, Tomato & Basil Soup 64
Leek, Sweet Potato & Chickpea Soup 66
Spiced Red Lentil Soup 67
Green Pea Soup & Easy Spring
Onion 'Focaccia' 68
Roast Pumpkin & Pasta Soup with Garlic,
Chilli & Thyme 72
Creamy Cauliflower & Garlic Soup 74
Spiced Couscous with Roasted Vegetables, Feta
& Pumpkin Seeds 122
Moroccan-Style Chicken Stew 126

Chickpeas
Leek, Sweet Potato & Chickpea Soup 66
Moroccan-Style Chicken Stew 126
Potato & Chickpea Curry with Spinach
& Coconut Milk 128
Tuna Steaks with Sweet Onions,
Spinach & Chickpeas 138

Cider vinegar
Rainbow Coleslaw 80
Beetroot, Goat's Cheese & Orange Salad 94
Pickled Summer Vegetables 98
Pasta & Bean Salad with Lemon
& Mint Dressing 118
Slow Cooked Smoky Pulled Pork 144
Winter Coleslaw 160

Cinnamon
Eggy Bread with Cinnamon Sugar 23
Cinnamon Swirl Cake 52
Potato & Chickpea Curry with Spinach
& Coconut Milk 128
Hot Orange & Grapefruit Punch 159
Tomato & Ginger Relish 164

Conchiglie
Conchiglie with Vegetable & Lentil Ragu 106

Conchigliette
Pasta & Bean Salad with Lemon
& Mint Dressing 118

Cornflour
Sea Salt & Butter Biscuits 38
Swiss-Style Cheese Fondue 142

Cornmeal
Cornbread 64

Courgette
Red Pepper, Tomato & Basil Soup 64
Rainbow Coleslaw 80
Tagliatelle with Smoked Salmon, Creme
Fraiche & Green Vegetables 114
Spiced Couscous with Roasted Vegetables, Feta
& Pumpkin Seeds 122
Ratatouille 136

Couscous
Spiced Couscous with Roasted Vegetables, Feta
& Pumpkin Seeds 122
Moroccan-Style Chicken Stew 126
Tuna Steaks with Sweet Onions,
Spinach & Chickpeas 138

Cream cheese
Apricot & Cream Cheese Pastries 32
Greek-Style Cheese Pie with Roast Sweet
Pepper & Cherry Tomato Salsa 84
Cheddar & Root Vegetable Crumble 152

Creme fraiche
Big Fluffy Pancakes 26
Banana & Choc Chip Drop Scones 30
Tagliatelle with Smoked Salmon, Creme
Fraiche & Green Vegetables 114
Sweet Onion & Potato Puff Pastry Tart 156
Lemon & Pine Nut Tart 172
Apple & Lemon Crumble 176

Cucumber
Smoked Mackerel Pâté 86
Yoghurt & Cucumber Dip with
Garlic & Dill 96

Damsons
Damson Brandy 162
Fruit Fools 180

Dark chocolate
Banana & Choc Chip Drop Scones 30
Mocha Brownies 44
Chocolate, Hazelnut & Oat Cookies 55
Glazed Chocolate & Almond Cake 174
Dark Chocolate & Cherry Crispy Cakes 182

Dark rum
Tiramisu 178

Dates
Oat Porridge with Dates, Walnuts
& Brown Sugar 19
Tomato & Ginger Relish 164

Edamame beans
Pasta & Bean Salad with Lemon
& Mint Dressing 118

Emmental
Swiss-Style Cheese Fondue 142

F

Fennel bulb
Pickled Summer Vegetables 98
Spaghetti with Sardines, Fennel & Lemon 110

Fennel seeds
Savoury Turkey Rolls & Rainbow Coleslaw 80
Pickled Summer Vegetables 98
Spaghetti with Sardines, Fennel & Lemon 110
Red Bean & Vegetable Goulash with
Dumplings & Soured Cream 146

Feta
Greek-Style Cheese Pie with Roast Sweet
Pepper & Cherry Tomato Salsa 84
Spiced Couscous with Roasted Vegetables, Feta
& Pumpkin Seeds 122

G

Ginger, ground
Gingerbread Biscuits with Royal Icing 42
Potato & Chickpea Curry with Spinach
& Coconut Milk 128

Ginger, root
Vegetable & Cashew Nut Stir-Fry 125
Salmon with Ginger, Lime,
Honey & Soy 134
Tomato & Ginger Relish 164

Gnocchi
Beef Ragu with Gnocchi 108

Goat's cheese
Beetroot, Goat's Cheese & Orange Salad 94

Golden syrup
Gingerbread Biscuits with Royal Icing 42
Chocolate, Hazelnut & Oat Cookies 55
Dark Chocolate & Cherry Crispy Cakes 182

Gorgonzola
Spirali with Butternut Squash,
Gorgonzola & Sage 112

Grapefruit
Hot Orange & Grapefruit Punch 159

Green beans
Baby Potato, Smoked Mackerel
& Tomato Salad 90
Beef Ragu with Gnocchi 108
Tagliatelle with Smoked Salmon, Creme
Fraiche & Green Vegetables 114
Pasta & Bean Salad with Lemon
& Mint Dressing 118

H

Haddock, smoked
Smoked Haddock & Sweetcorn Chowder 70

Halloumi
Oven-Baked Mushrooms, Halloumi &
Tomatoes on Sourdough Toast 20

Hazelnuts
Baked Apples with Hazelnuts,
Yoghurt & Honey 18
Chocolate, Hazelnut & Oat Cookies 55
Warm Spiced Nuts & Seeds 162

J

Jam sugar
Pineapple & Lime Marmalade 34

K

Kidney beans
Red Bean & Vegetable Goulash with
Dumplings & Soured Cream 146

L

Leeks
Leek, Sweet Potato & Chickpea Soup 66
Smoked Haddock & Sweetcorn Chowder 70
Cheddar & Root Vegetable Crumble 152

Lemon
Gingerbread Biscuits with Royal Icing 42
Very Lemony Drizzle Cake 48
Easy Rosemary & Sea Salt 'Focaccia' 56
Spiced Red Lentil Soup 67
Smoked Mackerel Pâté 86
Baby Potato, Smoked Mackerel
& Tomato Salad 90
Lemon Iced Tea 100
Spaghetti with Sardines, Fennel & Lemon 110
Tagliatelle with Smoked Salmon, Creme
Fraiche & Green Vegetables 114
Pasta & Bean Salad with Lemon
& Mint Dressing 118
Spiced Couscous with Roasted Vegetables, Feta
& Pumpkin Seeds 122
Moroccan-Style Chicken Stew 126
Roast Chicken with Sweet Potatoes, Lemon,
Honey & Thyme 148
Lemon & Pine Nut Tart 172
Apple & Lemon Crumble 176
Summer Fruit Pavlova 184

Lemon curd
Very Lemony Drizzle Cake 48
Lemon & Pine Nut Tart 172
Summer Fruit Pavlova 184

Lentils
Spiced Red Lentil Soup 67
Poached Chicken with Green Lentils,
Watercress & Mustard Dressing 88
Conchiglie with Vegetable & Lentil Ragu 106

Lime
Pineapple & Lime Marmalade 34
Vegetable & Cashew Nut Stir-Fry 125
Thai-Style Beef Salad with Noodles 130
Nachos with Black Beans, Avocado
& Sweetcorn Salsa 132
Salmon with Ginger, Lime,
Honey & Soy 134

Linguine
Linguine with Aubergine & Sun-Dried
Tomato Sauce 104
Spaghetti with Sardines, Fennel & Lemon 110

M

Maple syrup
Drop Scones with Bacon, Blueberries
& Maple Syrup 28

Mascarpone
Tiramisu 178

Minced beef
Beef Ragu with Gnocchi 108
Thai-Style Beef Salad with Noodles 130

Mushroom
Oven-Baked Mushrooms, Halloumi &
Tomatoes on Sourdough Toast 20
Beef Ragu with Gnocchi 108

Mustard
Cheese Scones 54
Chicken with Green Lentils, Watercress
& Mustard Dressing 88
Leafy Green Salad
with Vinaigrette Dressing 97
Winter Coleslaw 160

N

Nectarine
Summer Fruit Pavlova 184

Oats

Warming Porridge with Almonds
& Berry Compote 16
Oat Porridge with Dates, Walnuts
& Brown Sugar 19
Chocolate, Hazelnut & Oat Cookies 55

Orange

Almond & Orange Macaroons 40
Beetroot, Goat's Cheese & Orange Salad 94
Pickled Summer Vegetables 98
Hot Orange & Grapefruit Punch 159
Brown Sugar Meringues with Orange-Scented
Berries & Cream 168
Tiramisu 178

Pak choi

Vegetable & Cashew Nut Stir-Fry 125

Parmesan

Red Pepper, Tomato & Basil Soup 64
Linguine with Aubergine & Sun-Dried
Tomato Sauce 104
Conchiglie with Vegetable & Lentil Ragu
Beef Ragu with Gnocchi 108

Passata

Linguine with Aubergine & Sun-Dried
Tomato Sauce 104
Beef Ragu with Gnocchi 108
Red Bean & Vegetable Goulash with
Dumplings & Soured Cream 146
Braised Beef with Tomatoes & Red Wine 158

Peach

Fresh Fruit Milkshake 31
Summer Fruit Pavlova 184

Peas

Green Pea Soup & Easy Spring
Onion 'Focaccia' 68
Tagliatelle with Smoked Salmon, Creme
Fraiche & Green Vegetables 114
Cheddar & Root Vegetable Crumble 152
Saffron Risotto with Peas & Prawns 154

Pecans

Mocha Brownies 44

Penne

Broccoli, Ricotta & Tomato Pasta Salad 116

Pesto

Red Pepper, Tomato & Basil Soup 64

Pine nuts

Spaghetti with Sardines, Fennel & Lemon 110
Broccoli, Ricotta & Tomato Pasta Salad 116
Lemon & Pine Nut Tart 172

Pineapple

Pineapple & Lime Marmalade 34

Plum

Italian-Style Plum Cake 50
Fruit Fools 180

Polenta

Italian-Style Plum Cake 50
Cornbread 64
Cheesy Polenta with Smoky Beans 150
Braised Beef with Tomatoes & Red Wine 158

Pork shoulder

Slow Cooked Smoky Pulled Pork 144

Potatoes

Breakfast Potato Omelette 24
Leek, Sweet Potato & Chickpea Soup 66
Smoked Haddock & Sweetcorn Chowder 70
Savoury Turkey Rolls & Rainbow Coleslaw 80
Baby Potato, Smoked Mackerel
& Tomato Salad 90
Potato & Chickpea Curry with Spinach
& Coconut Milk 128
Ratatouille 136
Swiss-Style Cheese Fondue 142
Cheddar & Root Vegetable Crumble 152
Sweet Onion & Potato Puff Pastry Tart 156
Braised Beef with Tomatoes & Red Wine 158

Puff pastry

Apricot & Cream Cheese Pastries 32
Sweet Onion & Potato Puff Pastry Tart 156

Puffed rice cereal

Dark Chocolate & Cherry Crispy Cakes 182

Pumpkin

Roast Pumpkin & Pasta Soup with Garlic,
Chilli & Thyme 72

Pumpkin seeds

Spiced Couscous with Roasted Vegetables, Feta
& Pumpkin Seeds 122
Warm Spiced Nuts & Seeds 162

Quark

Smoked Mackerel Pâté 86

Raclette

Swiss-Style Cheese Fondue 142

Raisins

Spaghetti with Sardines, Fennel & Lemon 110

Raspberries

Warming Porridge with Almonds
& Berry Compote 16
Fresh Fruit Milkshake 31
Brown Sugar Meringues with Orange-Scented
Berries & Cream 168
Raspberry Clafoutis 170
Glazed Chocolate & Almond Cake 174
Fruit Fools 180
Summer Fruit Pavlova 184

Rhubarb

Rhubarb & Honey Muffins 46
Fruit Fools 180

Ricotta

Greek-Style Cheese Pie with Roast Sweet
Pepper & Cherry Tomato Salsa 84
Smoked Mackerel Pâté 86
Broccoli, Ricotta & Tomato Pasta Salad 116

Rigatoni

Broccoli, Ricotta & Tomato Pasta Salad 116

Risotto rice

Saffron Risotto with Peas & Prawns 154

Rocket leaves

White Bean Salad with Rosemary
& Garlic Dressing 92

Saffron

Moroccan-Style Chicken Stew 126
Saffron Risotto with Peas & Prawns 154

Sardines

Spaghetti with Sardines, Fennel & Lemon 110

Savoiardi biscuits

Tiramisu 178

Savoy cabbage

Red Bean & Vegetable Goulash with
Dumplings & Soured Cream 146

Shortcrust pastry

Savoury Turkey Rolls & Rainbow Coleslaw 80
Tuna & Tomato Pasties 82

Single cream
Creamy Cauliflower & Garlic Soup 74
Beetroot Soup 74
Spirali with Butternut Squash,
Gorgonzola & Sage 112
Raspberry Clafoutis 170

Smoked mackerel
Smoked Mackerel Pâté 86
Baby Potato, Smoked Mackerel
& Tomato Salad 90

Smoked salmon
Spinach & Cheese Scramble 22
Tagliatelle with Smoked Salmon, Creme
Fraiche & Green Vegetables 114

Sourdough
Oven-Baked Mushrooms, Halloumi &
Tomatoes on Sourdough Toast 20

Soured cream
Roast Pumpkin & Pasta Soup with Garlic,
Chilli & Thyme 72
Tagliatelle with Smoked Salmon, Creme
Fraiche & Green Vegetables 114
Nachos with Black Beans, Avocado
& Sweetcorn Salsa 132
Red Bean & Vegetable Goulash with
Dumplings & Soured Cream 146

Spaghetti
Roast Pumpkin & Pasta Soup with Garlic,
Chilli & Thyme 72
Spaghetti with Sardines, Fennel & Lemon 110

Spinach
Green Pea Soup & Easy Spring
Onion 'Focaccia' 68
Potato & Chickpea Curry with Spinach
& Coconut Milk 128
Tuna Steaks with Sweet Onions,
Spinach & Chickpeas 138
Roast Chicken with Sweet Potatoes, Lemon,
Honey & Thyme 148

Spirali
Spirali with Butternut Squash,
Gorgonzola & Sage 112

Sponge fingers
Tiramisu 178

Spring onion
Green Pea Soup & Easy Spring
Onion 'Focaccia' 68
Savoury Turkey Rolls & Rainbow Coleslaw 80
Pepper & Cherry Tomato Salsa 84
Baby Potato, Smoked Mackerel
& Tomato Salad 90
Pasta & Bean Salad with Lemon
& Mint Dressing 118

Vegetable & Cashew Nut Stir-Fry 125
Thai-Style Beef Salad with Noodles 130
Nachos with Black Beans, Avocado
& Sweetcorn Salsa 132

Squash
Roast Pumpkin & Pasta Soup with Garlic,
Chilli & Thyme 72
Spirali with Butternut Squash,
Gorgonzola & Sage 112
Red Bean & Vegetable Goulash with
Dumplings & Soured Cream 146
Cheddar & Root Vegetable Crumble 152

Strawberries
Brown Sugar Meringues with Orange-Scented
Berries & Cream 168
Summer Fruit Pavlova 184

Sun-dried tomato
Linguine with Aubergine & Sun-Dried Tomato
Sauce 104

Sunflower seeds
Warm Spiced Nuts & Seeds 162

Swede
Cheddar & Root Vegetable Crumble 152

Sweet potato
Leek, Sweet Potato & Chickpea Soup 66
Slow Cooked Smoky Pulled Pork 144
Red Bean & Vegetable Goulash with
Dumplings & Soured Cream 146
Roast Chicken with Sweet Potatoes,
Lemon, Honey & Thyme 148
Cheddar & Root Vegetable Crumble 152

Sweetcorn
Smoked Haddock & Sweetcorn Chowder 70
Nachos with Black Beans, Avocado
& Sweetcorn Salsa 132

Tenderstem broccoli
Broccoli, Ricotta & Tomato Pasta Salad 116

Tortilla chips
Nachos with Black Beans, Avocado
& Sweetcorn Salsa 132

Tuna
Tuna & Tomato Pasties 82
Tuna Steaks with Sweet Onions,
Spinach & Chickpeas 138

Turkey
Savoury Turkey Rolls & Rainbow Coleslaw 80
Turkey Chilli with Black Beans & Rice 124
Thai-Style Beef Salad with Noodles 130

Walnuts
Oat Porridge with Dates, Walnuts
& Brown Sugar 19
Mocha Brownies 44
Warm Spiced Nuts & Seeds 162

Watercress
Poached Chicken with Green Lentils,
Watercress
& Mustard Dressing 88

Wine, red
Beef Ragu with Gnocchi 108
Braised Beef with Tomatoes & Red Wine 158

Wine, white
Vegetable Stock 76
Chicken Stock 76
Poached Chicken with Green Lentils,
Watercress & Mustard Dressing 88
Spaghetti with Sardines, Fennel & Lemon 110
Swiss-Style Cheese Fondue 142
Saffron Risotto with Peas & Prawns 154

Whipping cream
Brown Sugar Meringues with Orange-Scented
Berries & Cream 168
Fruit Fools 180
Summer Fruit Pavlova 184

Yoghurt
Baked Apples with Hazelnuts,
Yoghurt & Honey 18
Big Fluffy Pancakes 26
Banana & Choc Chip Drop Scones 30
Yoghurt & Cucumber Dip with
Garlic & Dill 96